# MERSEY STARS

## An A-Z of Entertainers

## Michael Smout

**Published by** Sigma Leisure – an imprint of
Sigma Press, 1 South Oak Lane, Wilmslow, Cheshire SK9 6AR, England.

**British Library Cataloguing in Publication Data**
A CIP record for this book is available from the British Library.

**ISBN:** 1-85058-654-3

**Typesetting and Design by:** Sigma Press, Wilmslow, Cheshire.

**Printed by:** MFP Design & Print

**Cover Design:** The Agency, Macclesfield. Main picture: Paul McCartney. Other pictures, clockwise from top left: Arthur Askey, Billy Fury, Cilla Black, Kenny Everett, Ken Dodd, Jimmy Tarbuck

# Introduction

I arrived in Liverpool from darkest Herefordshire as a fresh faced curate in 1964. I had not been long in my first post at St Philemon's in Toxteth before I discovered the humour and music that makes Merseyside so special. It took me a little while to cotton on to people telling me that they went to different schools together or to a high school up a flight of steps. With the Beatles in full spate, music seemed to pervade the air.

My wife Val was born in Toxteth. Our children Paul and Katie spent their early years living in Newsham Park and Anfield Road. So I can claim some close Merseyside links. My later years of ministry have been as a vicar in Everton and Aughton.

This book is a tribute to the humour and music of Merseyside. Out of the hundreds eligible for entry, I have chosen those I think have some national claim to fame. If you think differently or have any corrections or additions to make, then please let me know, so that any second edition can be an improvement. I have written about the individual contributions of the Beatles, rather than recounting the story of the group yet again.

Thanks are due to a number of people for the help that they have given in this production. Keith Parkinson, Arthur and May Elliott and David Stuckey gave generously of their knowledge. Frank Loughlin and Stephen Shakeshaft of the Liverpool Daily Post and Echo, Peter Gaynor of Anfield Agency, Dennis Kelly, David Stuckey, Marion Hesketh and others came to the rescue with photographs. As usual, I have to thank Val for enduring my continuing love affair with my word processor.

*Michael Smout*

# The Entertainers – from A to Z

## Avril Angers (1921- )

Coming from a stage family often means that musical talent is inherited. Avril's father, Harry, was a professional comedian and her mother a dancer, Lillian Errol. She was born at a nursing home in Smithdown Road, but the family left the area six months later. At the age of 14 she was touring Yorkshire as a Tiller Girl in a stage show. Two years later she got a job as a comedienne at Minehead. At the audition she was asked what she did. 'I'm a comedienne,' she replied. 'What makes you think that?' Her response was to go through her routine. At its finish, the interviewer thought for a minute or so, looked at her and said, 'You're a comedienne.'

By now the Second World War was under way. Avril was a member of a party that went over to France to entertain the troops. In Amiens she was taken ill. For her, the tour was at an end. Soon she was asked to join ENSA, helping to entertain the troops in Sierra Leone and the Gold Coast. This earned her the Africa Star. Here she met up with one of her brothers, Julian, who at the time was a RAF radio operator. It was a life of travel and excitement. Next she was in Cairo, where the party did a show at the Opera House, with King Farouk in the audience. From there, it was onto El Alamein to help the celebrations of the decisive battle of 1942. After visits to Tripoli and Cyprus, it was back to London after an absence of two years.

Back home, work with the BBC soon came Avril's way on such programmes as 'Monday Night at Eight' and 'Variety Bandbox'. She joined Cyril Fletcher in a review at the Palace Theatre, London. They had to compete with air raids, so the show closed after two weeks. Next she worked with Max Wall at the Duchess Theatre. Carroll Levis was looking for someone to be with him on his TV discovery show. He chose Avril, who became known to millions of viewers. She also starred with Levis in a film 'The Lucky Mascot'. To her amazement, in 1947 she was chosen to represent the country at the United Nations Ball in Berlin. On radio, she appeared in 'Variety Bandbox',

'Merry-Go Round' and 'Monday Night at Eight'. Her stage career flourished, acting first of all as stand in for Joy Nicholls in the 'Take It From Here' stage production and also for Bud Flanagan at the Victoria Palace. Then she went on to star in 'Blithe Spirit' and 'Hobson's Choice' amongst a series of hit performances. In films, 'The Green Man' with Alistair Sim and 'The Family Way' with Hayley Mills established Avril as a serious actress as well as a comedienne.

Avril often came back to Liverpool, sometimes in a professional role. For example, she appeared in 'I'll Get My Man' at the Royal Court in April 1967, alongside fellow-Liverpudlian Anthony Booth. On other occasions, she came for family visits. Her sister Audrey played a large part in the starting of the Liverpool Spastic Fellowship at its Angers House Headquarters.

# Arthur Askey (1900-82)

In the days of the Liverpool trams, the cry of the conductor, 'Aythangyew,' was heard just before he rang the bell to alert the passengers that the vehicle was about to move. It was a word that was to be associated with Arthur Askey, along with 'Before your very eyes' and the greeting at the start of his act 'Hello, playmates'.

The Holy Land of Toxteth has no particular religious connections. It is simply a local description of a group of streets of terraced houses wedged between Park Road and Mill Street. They are named after Old Testament characters – Moses, Isaac, Jacob and David. It was on 6 June 1900, in the final years of the reign of Queen Victoria, that Arthur Bowden Askey was born at 19 Moses Street. Arthur joked, many years later, 'They've got a plaque on the wall that tells the whole romantic legend in one word – Condemned.' Fortunately he was wrong. 19 Moses Street still stands today.

Arthur's father, Samuel, was a general merchant's bookkeeper, married to Betsy. After the birth of Arthur, the family was completed by the arrival of a sister, Irene. In later years, she was a good pianist. Arthur had only six months experience of the Holy Land. The family moved on to 90 Rosslyn Street, Aigburth and, 10 years later, a few blocks down to 58 Sandhurst Street.

After attending St Michael's-in-the-Hamlet Church of England Primary School, Arthur gained a scholarship at the Liverpool Institute in Mount Street. Many are the links of coincidence in history, but none more so than the fact that Paul McCartney sat in the same desk at the school 40 years later. When Arthur was called upon to present McCartney with a record award, Paul sent him a telegram saying, 'Many congratulations from the fellow who inherited your desk at school. You carved your name with pride and it is still there'

St Michael's-in-the-Hamlet parish church is one of the two cast-iron churches in Liverpool. The other is St George's, Everton. In those pre-radio and TV days, church was not only a place for worship, but also for recreation and community events. Arthur took part in the Sunday school and Bible classes, but his greatest enjoyment was singing in the church choir. Eventually he became head-chorister. His supreme moment came when he was asked to join a choir, selected from the best of the church singers in the Liverpool area. Its job was to sing at the opening of the Lady Chapel, the first part of the vast Anglican Cathedral on St James's Mount to be completed. It was to act as a mini-cathedral for the next sixty years or so until the whole edifice was finished. King Edward VII had laid the foundation stone on 19 July 1904. Now on St Peter's Day, 29 June 1910, Arthur had the privilege of being one of the soloists to perform before a packed congregation of ecclesiastical and civic dignitaries. He called it 'my most memorable performance'.

From such dizzy heights he returned to the everyday round of school life. His first amateur appearance on stage had been at the Aigburth Road Assemby Rooms (later the Rivoli Cinema). It was possible, Arthur discovered, to get a few afternoons off by singing in one of the concert parties. These were to provide entertainment for the troops stationed around Merseyside during the First World War. On a few occasions he found himself performing alongside Tommy Handley, another product of the Holy Land. During these years, he picked up the name by which he was known during his stage and broadcasting years – 'Big-Hearted Arthur'. He played a lot of cricket at the St Michael's recreation ground. Whenever the ball was hit for six, he always volunteered to be the one to retrieve it. 'Big Hearted Arthur, that's me,' he used to say. The sobriquet changed to 'Big Hearted Martha' whenever he was in pantomime.

At the Institute, Arthur excelled at geography and history, but his future career was more than hinted at by his participation in school

*Big Hearted Arthur Askey*

plays and a prize won for singing. When eventually his voice broke, he made comic songs the main part of his act. From the age of 16, he worked at the Liverpool Education Offices at 14 Sir Thomas Street. 'Tonsils and adenoids' was the name he gave to his particular sphere of operation. Apparently this meant he was responsible for handing out official documents to the parents of children due to have operations. These eight years of hard labour were only interrupted by a few months of army service in the Welsh Regiment. He was fortunate enough to be called up just six months before the end of the war. When asked if he had served overseas, he replied, 'Yes, in the Far East – Great Yarmouth.'

Around the same time, love was in the air. His girlfriend, May Swash, worked at Goodlass, Wall & Co. in the Strand. Every morning, they travelled in to work together by train from St Michael's to Central Station. She was the one who persuaded him to give up the security of the job with the Council to become a professional entertainer. Every time the collection came round for the retirement of yet another council stalwart, Arthur felt decreasingly inclined to spend the rest of his working life in the confines of Sir Thomas Street. He used his spare time collecting jokes from concert parties in such places as the Olympian Gardens, Rock Ferry and, whilst on holiday, watching the Jovial Jesters Pierrots at Rhyl. After winning various talent contests, he started a concert party of his own called 'The Filberts'. Then May persuaded him to take the risk of giving in his notice.

For most of his first year as a professional he was with the Song Salad Concert Party on tour, starting at the Electric Theatre, Colchester. Arthur was rarely to return to Liverpool after this. His first professional appearance in Liverpool was not until May 1939, when he appeared at the Empire in the touring 'Bandwaggon' show. The highlight of the following year was his marriage to May on 23 March at St Michael-in-the Hamlet church. They were to have one daughter, Anthea, an actress, and three grandchildren.

Over the next decade, Arthur, having moved to live in London, earned a decent income on the after-dinner speaker circuit and in pantomimes. So much so that he did not need to undertake stage tours. The big breakthrough came at the beginning of 1938. He was asked to star in the BBC series 'Bandwaggon' along with Richard Murdoch, starting on 5 January. It was the first comedy series to have a regular weekly spot and a scriptwriter. The characters, including Mrs. Bagwash, her daughter Nausea and Lewis the goat, were located in a flat in the BBC buildings. The author George Bernard Shaw once told Arthur that the programme was schoolboy rubbish. Arthur responded by asking Shaw if he could do an impersonation of him on the programme. In reply, Shaw sent a postcard with the one word 'No' on it. Never defeated, Arthur then went to see Shaw personally, somehow getting assent. Arthur then appeared as a Shaw lookalike, complete with beard, Norfolk jacket and knickerbockers. On being asked, 'Are you Shaw?' he responded, 'No, I'm certain'. The series ended on 12 July 1939, when Murdoch was called up.

The spin off from 'Bandwaggon' was more work offers than Arthur could take. A staple part of his act was the Busy Bee Song, which became popular when he performed it on 'Bandwaggon'. The partnership with Richard Murdoch continued in films such as 'The Ghost Train', 'Bandwaggon', 'I Thank You' and 'Charley's Big Hearted Aunt'.

The first TV series 'Before Your Very Eyes' was in February 1953, but still Arthur was in great demand on the stage. After four years with ITV, he swapped to BBC TV, introducing the voluptuous blonde Sabrina in his series. He had dangerous moments, such as when he fell through a trapdoor at the Palladium in 1967 and off the stage at Clacton Pier Theatre in 1976. It was a proud moment in his life when he was awarded the OBE in 1969. The Variety Club celebrated his 50 years in the business in 1974. This same year came a sad personal blow with the death of May, after a period of mental illness. Shy all her life, she did not feel able even to go to Royal Command Performances. Some felt the strain of being married to a well-known personality had hastened her death.

Arthur continued to perform, now living with his sister Irene in Kensington. Over the following years his health deteriorated, including two heart attacks. Like the trouper he was he vowed, 'I'll keep working, but if I don't get laughs, I'll retire.' 1981 was the year he was made CBE, as well as the year of his last appearance in a pantomime, at Richmond. In June 1982, having collapsed, he was taken to hospital. His left leg had to be amputated, followed by the other in October. His determination showed in his reading of scripts for the time when he came out of hospital. On 16 November 1982, Big Hearted Arthur, the diminutive man with the bottle-lens glasses, died in hospital.

# Thomas Beecham (1879-1961)

Beecham's Pills had made a fortune for the Beecham family. Thomas, senior, came to live in St Helens in 1858. Until then he had travelled the length and breadth of Lancashire, selling herbal remedies. At one stage he had lodgings in Circus Street, Liverpool, while he sold his pills in Whitechapel. Now he started to make his own pills in his garden shed. The business was so successful that a decade or two later he had built his own factory. His son Joseph and his wife Josephine set up home in Westfield Street, where two daughters were born. Soon after moving to Arthur Street in 1878, Thomas junior was born on 22 April 1879. As the family business expanded, so the family homes got larger. In 1885 the move was made to Ewansville, a large house in the Blacklow Brow area of Huyton.

Joseph was fond of music, having an organ at home. Once he tried to plug in a new machine called an orchestrion, only to plunge Huyton into darkness when the lights fused. Later he had another house built in Arkwright Street, big enough to house a concert hall.

Little wonder then that the young Thomas took to music. By the age of six, he was being taught by a local organist. After going to a school in a house next door to his own, Thomas was sent to Rossall public school, near Blackpool, in 1892. Here music lessons continued. Soon he could play any Beethoven sonata by sight. From Rossall, Wadham College, Oxford was the next stop. Eighteen months of the three-year course was enough for Thomas. He did discover, however, that he had a photographic memory. Sixty years later he could remember the page and line upon which quotations were found in books. He returned home to help run the family business.

Back home, it was soon obvious that Thomas was little interested in pills. Instead, he spent most of his time organising the musical scene in St Helens. In 1899 he founded the St Helens Orchestral Society. His father was Mayor of St Helens that year. To celebrate the event, the Hallé Orchestra had agreed to give a concert, to be conducted by Richter. At the last moment, the renowned conductor fell ill. Thomas stepped into the breach, without the opportunity of a rehearsal. The 20-year-old conducted the whole performance from memory.

Besides being Lord Mayor, Joseph had an eye for the ladies. So much so that his wife and daughter Emily refused to go to any of his official functions. A family row erupted when Joseph had his wife admitted to an asylum. Thomas and Emily had to take their father to court to find out where she was and get her released. Divorce soon followed. This did not put Thomas off marriage. In 1903 he married Utica Welles, an American doctor's daughter.

The family business fortune meant that Thomas could devote himself to his musical activities without worrying about earning an income. He received no academic musical training, expressing his dislike of colleges. Some accused him of being no more than an amateur. In 1905, he gave his first professional performance in London with 40 members of the Queen's Hall Orchestra. Two years later, he started the Beecham Symphony Orchestra. The members were known as much for the pranks they got up to as for the music they performed. It became known as the 'Fireworks Orchestra', because whenever it passed through Crewe station on its travels, fireworks were let off through the train windows. It was one of Thomas's party tricks to drop bags of light bulbs down the lift-shafts of hotels at which the orchestra stayed.

It was a case of like father, like son, when, in October 1909, Thomas was named in the divorce proceedings of a Mrs Maud Foster, having to stump up £3,000 in costs. In 1912 he separated from his wife Utica. Two years later, Thomas gave up the orchestra to form the Beecham Opera Company. By 1923 this had become the British National Opera Company. His father had made an enormous outlay to buy a large area of Covent Garden, which included the Opera House and two theatres. Although he was knighted for services to music in 1916, Thomas soon found himself having to work full-time to refinance his father's debts. But all to no avail. By 1932 he was bankrupt. Thomas was not one to give up easily. When the BBC started its own symphony orchestra without his help, he set up his own – the London Philharmonic Orchestra.

During the years of the Second World War, Thomas conveniently escaped to the USA, Canada and Australia, conducting many different orchestras. At this time, it was his love life which made the headlines as much as his music. He was followed to New York by Lady Cunard, whose passion for him was not mutual. To her great alarm, Thomas met up with Betty Humby, a concert pianist he had known for many years before. Both by now having been divorced, they married in New York in September 1943.

Back in England after the war, Thomas was told that the London Philharmonic Orchestra no longer required his services. His response, in typical Beecham fashion, was to start another orchestra, the Royal Philharmonic, naturally known as the Pill-armonic. In 1949 he conducted a 70th-birthday celebratory concert at the Philharmonic Hall in Liverpool. He gave his opinion that the Liverpool Philharmonic Orchestra is 'the best-conducted musical society in the world'. Years earlier at the Philharmonic, Thomas was conducting when a new first trumpet player made his debut. Being a brass band player he could not transpose music, so he played very quietly at rehearsals. Thomas gave him some private tuition, saying, 'Keep your eye on me and I'll keep my eye on you.' The player was Harry Mortimer, later to be one of the greatest names in the brass band world. When Thomas was on the selection panel for a new orchestra he said, 'I want the man who plays the trumpet at Liverpool. He's very awkward, but he's very good.'

In the immediate post-war years, the general administrator at Covent Garden was David Webster. He had been in charge of a big Liverpool department store and chairman of the Philharmonic. He gave a very critical review of an opera Beecham produced in Liverpool. Thomas replied, 'And who is this David Webster? I insist that all copies of the offending newspaper be burned on St George's steps and Mr. Webster with them.' It was little wonder that Thomas was excluded from Covent Garden as long as Webster was in charge.

His second wife having died in 1957, Thomas married 27-year-old Shirley Hudson two years later. The last Beecham concert was given at the Guildhall, Portsmouth on 7 May 1960. He died, after a heart attack, in March 1961. Burial took place at Brookwood cemetery in Surrey.

A conductor of world ranking, Thomas was either loved or hated by his critics. He always spoke his mind. For example, he got to the end of a Vaughan Williams piece at a rehearsal, but he kept on conducting. He then asked the leader of the orchestra why it had stopped playing. 'It's finished,' came the reply. 'Thank God for that,' he said. When asked if he had played any Stockhausen, he famously replied,"No, but I have trodden in some." A soprano, on learning The Messiah, told him, 'The score goes with me everywhere, to work, to meals, up to bed at night,' he responded, 'Then I trust we may look forward to an immaculate conception.'

A man of immense energy, needing only three hours sleep a night, Thomas founded, financed and conducted five orchestras, built up an opera company, and made numerous recordings.

# Billy Bennett (1887-1942)

'Almost a Gentleman' was the title associated with Billy during his music hall career. Although born in Glasgow, the family moved to Liverpool in his early years. His father John was a comedian. He was half of a duo, Bennett and Martell, who made many appearances at the Drury Lane Theatre in London.

Billy started his education at Clint Road School. Then he went on to Earle Road, where he later gave money for book prizes for the pupils. After attempting to be an insurance salesman, he decided to follow in his father's footsteps on to the stage. He began as the rear end of a pantomime horse, progressing to become an acrobat. The outbreak of war in 1914 found him joining the 16th Lancers. Although he never spoke about his experiences in later years, his service was distinguished. He was awarded the DCM, Military Medal and the Croix de Guerre. Wounded at the battle of Mons, he found himself in a French field hospital. To fill in the time, he formed with Mark Lupino the Shell Fire Concert Party.

This training stood Billy in good stead after the war. He started doing a trench comedian's act, dressed in full uniform. The second time was to be at the Theatre Royal, Dublin. The manager suggested that a military act in Ireland was not the wisest thing to do. So Billy improvised with the help of a false moustache. Soon his costume had changed to the one for which he is best remembered: quiff, moustache, top hat, dicky bow, dinner jacket and boots. In the latter years of the 1920s, he started to make recordings of his stage songs and recitations, such as 'A Sailor's Farewell to his Horse' and 'The Tight Brigade'.

In August 1928, Billy went to New York on a three-year contract. He lasted only three months. The heat affected him so much that he had to return home. From 1930, he was Mose, in a duo, Alexander and Mose, an act for which they blacked up. Alexander was played first by James Carew and then by Albert Whelan. In later years, Carew took over his original role again. On radio, Billy made over 300 broadcasts for the BBC.

Taken ill during the first performance of 'Black Varieties' at the Opera House in Blackpool, Billy never appeared on stage again. He died in May 1942. Rumbustious on the stage, he was very shy off it. He never married. He was a very sociable person, being in great demand as an after-dinner speaker.

# Cilla Black (1943- )

She really does say 'gorra lorra' was the surprised comment of an interviewer, who was trying to discover whether or not Cilla spoke with her Scouse accent in real life. Of all the Liverpool entertainers, Cilla is the one that some Liverpudlians love to have a go at. This is because they either think that she has deserted the city or puts on an exaggerated Scouse accent on her TV programmes. This all reached a peak in May 1994, when the students of John Moores University (most of whom do not come from Liverpool) protested against the award to her of an honorary degree. Local people interviewed at the time made comments such as, 'She's made her way and left,' and, 'She's done nothing for the life of the city.' The university authorities pointed out that the degree was not an academic award, while Cilla herself responded, 'I've graduated from the University of Life.' Since some of the other Liverpool stars had left the city over the years, it may have something to do with the fact that she is one of the few local women entertainers who have succeeded.

Born on 23 May 1943 in Stanley Hospital, she was christened Priscilla Maria Veronica White. The family lived at 380 Scotland Road, adjacent to a Chinese laundry. Her father worked on the docks and her mother had a market stall in St Martin's. Such was the claustrophobia of city life that the first time she ever saw the countryside was when she went pea-picking in Lydiate at the age of 14. She left St Anthony's school with a report indicating that she was best suited for office work. That is exactly what she did. After Anfield Commercial College, she worked for a cable company as a typist. In the evenings she acted as a cloakroom attendant at the Cavern. Doing this enabled her to get into the lunchtime sessions for nothing to listen to the Beatles, Gerry and the Pacemakers and the other up-and-coming groups on the Merseyside scene.

Cilla did her singing at the Iron Door club in Temple Street. When the Beatles were playing there one night, she was allowed to sing by popular request. It was John Lennon who suggested that Brian Epstein, the Beatles manager, should hear her. He did. Immediately he signed her up, predicting a great future for her. [She made her professional debut in Southport with the Beatles.] At his suggestion, Cilla changed her name from White to Black. She also had a part-time job on the coffee bar at the Zodiac Club, a meeting place for local musicians. It was here she first met and fell in love with Bobby Willis, a bakery worker and a talented singer in his own right. He wrote 'Sky of Love', which was the B-side of 'Love of the Lovers'. Brian Epstein insisted that the romance should be kept quiet, because he thought it might not go down too well with her fans. She and Bobby eventually married at Marylebone Registry Office on 25 January 1969, with another ceremony taking place at St Mary's Roman Catholic Church in Woolton later on.

Cilla's first single, 'Love of the Lovers', made the lower reaches of the charts. Her second attempt 'Anyone who had a Heart' made it to the top. 'You're My World' and 'Alfie' continued the run of success. This all led on to a TV series, 'Step Inside Love'. She took part in the 1964 Royal Variety Performance, as well as appearing over 400 times at the Palladium. Then, in 1968, came a film, 'Work Is a Four-Letter Word'. A complete flop, it was followed by a period when little work came in. Some wondered if Cilla's short career was at an end. It was saved by Terry Wogan. Cilla had decided, along with Bobby, her manager since the death of Brian Epstein in 1967, to produce an album of her hit songs. She hoped that this would revive her flagging career. Since most TV chat shows are used to promote records or books, Cilla took the opportunity to appear on the Wogan show in 1983. The way she talked with such zest impressed the TV bosses. Cilla puts this down to having spent so much of the time before back in Liverpool, listening to Billy Butler on local radio.

*Cilla Black – success was no surprise*

The producers of a new programme 'Surprise, Surprise' were looking for a compere. They gave Cilla the job, thus starting her subsequent career as a presenter rather than a singer. There was a surprise of the wrong sort when she was taken ill during the programme in June 1984. Fortunately, a minor operation put matters right. A little more excitement occurred in December 1985 when she sued EMI and British Rail for using some of the 'Step Inside' music in an advert. Her performance in 'Surprise, Surprise' made Cilla the obvious choice for 'Blind Date'. This was originally an Australian idea. There was some opposition to this type of programme being shown, so it needed a compere who could make sure that it never went over the top. Except for the fact that it was discovered that an early contestant was already married, the programme became an instant and enduring hit.

Thirty years in show business were celebrated in 1993. To mark the event an autobiographical TV show included her early Liverpool life. There was even more cause for celebration when Cilla was awarded the OBE in July 1997. She is still in great demand on TV, hosting the challenge show 'The Moment of Truth'.

The TV image of Cilla is of the homely, ordinary Liverpool lass, just chatting away as if she had met someone in the street. She has achieved this by being completely professional. Without this, it is doubtful if the successive list of shows would have had any success. Family life has always been of the utmost importance to her. In 1973 she decided that she would work for only six months in the year for the sake of the family. Working closely with Bobby helped towards a long marriage. He was willing to sacrifice his potential singing career to manage Cilla's interests. So close were the two that Bobby always sat in on interviews that Cilla gave, because once she was molested when being interviewed alone. She was completely devastated by his death from cancer at the Royal Free Hospital in London on 23 October 1999.

Success has brought a house in Denham that stands in 17 acres of grounds, bought in 1965. Pride in their children, Robert (born 1970), Ben (born 1974) and Jack (born 1980) was only saddened by losing a baby daughter. In 1975 Cilla gave birth to a daughter Helen who died shortly after due to a lung defect. For Cilla, as with any mother, this was a crushing blow. Val Doonican was standing in for her in a show in Coventry, to which Cilla returned two weeks later. She suffered a time of deep depression. It needed friends like Jimmy Tarbuck and Frankie Howerd, as well as the family, to help her get back to something like her normal self. At the time she said, 'I have fallen out of friends with God.' In 1991 there was further anxiety when Robert was involved in a car crash. One of the signs of the financial distance between Scotland Road and Denham was the sending of the children to Merchant Taylors' School in Northwood, London – in Liverpool days all the children of rich parents used to go to Merchant Taylors' School in Crosby.

Being a red-haired girl singer in Liverpool at the time of the Beatles was perhaps the bit of luck that every budding artist needs. If Cilla had lived, say, in Birmingham, who knows if she would ever have been heard of. But given that start, her long career has been based on hard work and endeavour. Her stage appearances in Liverpool have not been frequent, although she was in pantomime at the Empire in 1979 and 1986. In October 1989 she opened the St John's Centre, refurbished after a disastrous fire. It is wrong to say that she has done little for the city. For example in 1992, only two years before the protest of the John Moores University students, she had helped to launch an appeal for the plastic surgery and burns unit at Alder Hey Children's Hospital. Her long absences from Liverpool have been simply because, particularly in the early days of a seven-hour car journey, London is the centre of the entertainment world. Especially for those involved in TV, that is where they need to be.

# Stan Boardman (1942- )

When any Merseysider hears mention of the 'Jeermans', Stan immediately springs to mind. His Scouse accent and humour have enabled him to become one of the most popular of local comedians. He was a late starter in the world of comedy. He was 34 years old when he won

Stan Boardman (right) and friend clocking up more laughs

the national final of a Butlin's talent show at the London Palladium. His family home was originally in the Scotland Road area, until the house was hit by a bomb in 1942. The move was made to Kirkdale. Since leaving school he had had jobs as a pipe fitter, welder, beach photographer and lifeguard, having done National Service in the Royal Engineers in 1960. Finally he had worked in haulage at Huyton, without much success. It was while on the dole in 1976 that he had scraped together enough money to take the family for a few days holiday at Butlin's. While there, the family, wife Vivienne and children Andrea and Paul, dared him to take part in the camp's talent show. He did so well that he eventually found himself in the national finals.

Stan made his professional debut at Bromborough British Legion, had a summer show in Lowestoft in 1982 and was at the Liverpool Empire in 1985. He came to national notice with 10 appearances on 'The Comedians'. He was then given his own Saturday night TV show, 'The Video Entertainers'. Other appearances were in 'Opportunity Knocks' and 'Seaside Special'. One of his less happy memories of the time was going with Russell Harty to record a show on the Forties Bravo oil rig out in the North Sea. Whilst on board a storm arose, leaving them stranded for some days. Although not seen as much on TV these days, Stan is in great demand on the club circuit.

# Tony Booth (1932-)

Probably better known as Prime-Minister Tony Blair's son-in-law, Tony made his name in the cult TV series of the 1960s 'Till Death Us Do Part'. In this he played the role of 'The Scouse Git', Alf Garnett's son-in-law. Born in central Liverpool, he has hit the headlines as much for his private life as for his acting. He has been married four times, the most well known of which was his third wife, Pat Phoenix, a star of 'Coronation Street'. Tony married her shortly before her death from cancer. In 1998 he married his fourth wife, Stephanie Buckley, for whom it was a fifth marriage.

# Adrian Boult (1889-1983)

The least flamboyant of all symphony orchestra conductors, Adrian Boult and Thomas Beecham dominated the English classical music scene of the middle part of the century. The austere, bald, moustached figure became well known in concert halls up and down the country, as well as abroad. Conducting until past his 90th birthday, his style showed no emotion. With a minimal swing of the baton, he somehow managed to produce sublime music from the orchestras in his charge. The first two years of Adrian's life were spent in Chester. He was born at 4 Abbots Hayes, Liverpool Road in that city. His father Cedric, an oil merchant, and mother Katherine were strong Unitarians, a faith which Adrian continued throughout his life. In 1891 the family moved to Brooke House, Blundellsands. Adrian's father travelled by train into Liverpool, his work now being involved with shipping and Valvoline Oil. The first concert that the young Adrian, a musical prodigy, was taken to at the Philharmonic Hall was on 26 October 1895. In 1901 he was transferred from the dame school in Blundellsands to board at Westminster School in London.

On 28 July 1904 the family made another move. This time it was to The Abbey Manor in West Kirby. Adrian left Westminster School in 1908 to go on to Christ Church, Oxford. Here he was so busy with his music and theatre that his degree in history suffered badly. At the outbreak of war Adrian wanted to enlist, but was prevented from doing so by a heart condition. He did his bit by helping to drill the 16th Service Battalion of the King's Liverpool Regiment in West Kirby. He moved on with them when they were transferred to Kinmel Park near St Asaph in Wales.

Many orchestral players were of an age to join up. This meant that those left were unemployed, because their orchestras were now in limbo. Adrian decided to help to solve the problem. On 27 October 1914, at the Public Hall in West Kirby, he conducted an orchestra consisting of the combined remaining members of the Liverpool Philharmonic and Hallé Orchestras. This was such a success that he then undertook a series of concerts in Liverpool. Starting at the 4000-seater Sun Hall in Kensington, they were eventually transferred to the David Lewis Club in Great George Place.

Adrian soon moved to London to work in the War Office. Having taken a doctor of music degree in 1914, he was appointed after the war to the staff of the Royal College of Music. In the same year, he took over as the conductor of the recently formed British Symphony Orchestra. During these years he had conducted two concerts at the Liverpool Philharmonic Hall. The first had been on 25 January 1916 and the second a concert with the great cellist Pablo Casals on 15 November 1921.

Adrian's father retired through ill health in 1922. The family moved from West Kirby to Northlands at Landford near Salisbury. From 1924 to 1930 Adrian was musical director of the City of Birmingham Orchestra, which had been founded four years previously. Lord Reith, head of the BBC, then appointed him Director of Music and conductor of the BBC Symphony Orchestra. Adrian held the post for 20 years. He was knighted for his services to music in 1937. When he left, after a somewhat acrimonious dispute in 1950, he became freelance. His career broadened out to encompass more recording and conducting many different orchestras. For the first nine years he was musical director of the London Philharmonic Orchestra. During most of the previous years he had been closely connected with the Promenade Concerts at the Royal Albert Hall. Until he was past 90 Adrian was kept very busy, except for some lean years from 1961 to 1965.

Adrian died at a London nursing home on 20 February 1983. There was no funeral because he had donated his body to medical research. His great achievement as a conductor had been to bring to the fore the works of English composers such as Edward Elgar and Ralph Vaughan-Williams.

# Faith Brown (1944- )

Sheer embarrassment brought Faith the greatest opportunity of her life. She was in the middle of her act at the Orrell Park Ballroom when her dress split. To distract the attention of the audience, she went into an impersonation of Hylda Baker. An agent, Byron Godfey, realised how talented Faith was. He immediately signed her up.

Born Irene Carroll in Walton on 28 May 1944, Faith used to do impersonations of the teachers at school. On leaving, she worked as a shop assistant at Lewis's, selling china and doing oven cleaner demonstrations. Even then she entertained customers with her mimicking. She starting singing in 1962, her debut being with Hal Graham's band at the Rialto in Toxteth. A group called The Carrolls was then formed, consisting of Faith and three of her four brothers. They became well known on the northern club circuit. The name Faith Brown was taken when she left the group to go solo. The manager was Len Waty, whom she later married. Their daughter Danielle was born in 1978.

A contract with Thames TV led to an appearance in 'Who Do You Do?' and a one-off show 'The Faith Brown Awards'. TV work meant that the family had to move to the Slough area. A six-week series followed called 'The Faith Brown Chat Show'. In each show she did interviews with five well-known people, each one of whom she was impersonating. In 1980, Faith won the TV Times Award for the funniest woman on TV. Two years later she was the subject of 'This Is Your Life'. The latter part of her career has been devoted to serious acting.

# Dora Bryan (1923- )

Born in Southport on 7 February 1923, Dora soon moved to Oldham with the family. She made her first appearance in pantomime in 1935, joining the repertory company in Oldham two years later. She has had a distinguished career on the stage, in TV and in films. On stage she excelled in the classical and in musicals ranging from 'The Merry Wives of Windsor' to 'Charlie Girl'. On TV, she has many credits including 'Dora' and 'Foxy Lady'. Her best remembered film is 'A Taste of Honey', for which she won an academy award, but she also starred in 'The Great St Trinian's Train Robbery' and 'The Blue Lamp'. Dora is married to William Lawson, with a daughter Georgina.

# Billy Butler (1942- )

'Mrs Butler's Eldest' has been a lynchpin of Merseyside local radio entertainment since 1971. Billy was born in Salem Street, Amlwch, Anglesey on 24 January 1942. His father Frank was a heavy goods vehicle driver, who died when Billy was 12 years of age. This left his mother Gladys to bring up the family. She died in 1993. After the move to Liverpool, the family lived at 52 Grey Rock Street. Billy was educated at Whitefield Road School until 1953 and the Liverpool Collegiate until 1958. After jobs as a plumber and then a dock clerk, he got a foothold in the entertainment world by passing an audition for a TV show in 1961, which led to his being in 'Thank Your Lucky Stars' for two years. After spells with the Merseybeats, Tuxedos, Hangman and Cherry Pickers groups, he was a DJ at the Cavern for five years from 1964, as well as compere at Mardi Gras, Downbeats, Victoriana, Blue Angel and other venues. He then sang with the Merseybeats, before taking up his radio career. With his colleague, Wally Scott, Billy has had two spells each with BBC Radio Merseyside, (1971 to 1978 and 1984 to 1995) and Radio City (Magic 1548) (1979 to 1983 and 1995 to 1999). In addition to the staple morning programmes, the weekly 'Hold Your Plums' programme became equally popular. Beyond this, he has appeared in numerous shows, often for charity, around the area, including a panto season at the Empire Theatre. A weekly late evening music programme on national BBC radio in 1984-86, plus the occasional TV appearances such as 'Fax' and 'Live on Two', showed that it was not easy to translate a Liverpool style to a national wavelength. It also demonstrated that he functions best in partnership with Wally Scott in an informal setting. On local TV he has appeared in 'Billy and Wally's Big Night Out' and other shows. Writing opportunities came with a column in the Liverpool Echo from 1981 to 1989 and 1995 until 1997.

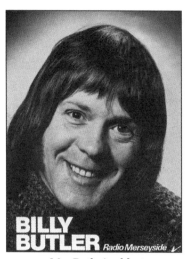

*Mrs Butler's eldest*

Moments of high drama on radio have included a row in August 1988 because of remarks Billy made about the budget. Again in October 1998 he defied orders not to play a Cliff Richard Top Ten hit. Marriage took place to Carol at Huyton in 1964. They have four sons, Stewart, Lee, David and Paul. On divorce, Billy's second marriage, to Lesley, took place on 10 August 1991 at St James's Church, New Brighton, with a reception following at Edge House Hotel. Over the years, Billy has won many DJ and Personality of the Year Awards, culminating with a Sony Radio Award in 1998. 2000 saw his return to Radio Merseyside with the Billy Butler show.

# Keith Chegwin (1957- )

Alcoholism, the curse of many an entertainer, dragged Keith from the dizzy heights of TV fame to the depths of despair. Little did the boy star think in those early days that one day life would be such a struggle.

Mr and Mrs Chegwin got two for the price of one when Keith and his identical twin Jeff were born at Walton Hospital on 17 January 1957. The family home was at 37 Aintree Road, Bootle. Father worked at a job in a timber merchants. It is probably not a coincidence that he spent much of his spare time doing jobs around the house. Mother had a part-time job in a shoe shop. Keith was a member of the local church choir, enjoying the money more than the singing. He also had a short-term relationship with the Scouts and the St John's Ambulance. He got up to quite a few pranks at St George of England school in Bootle. Once, in the winter, he turned the thermostat on the school boiler down. It was assumed to have broken down, so the school was closed for the rest of the day. On another occasion, he tried to gain the affections of a girl by giving her some flowers. Unfortunately they were daffodils he had pinched from Derby Park. Even more unfortunately, the park keeper saw him. He was reported to the headmaster.

From putting on his own shows at home, Keith decided to enter a talent show in Rhyl, which he won. He then joined a concert party called the Happy Wanderers, who went round entertaining in hospitals and nursing homes in Lancashire. Next he joined up with Jeff and his sister Janice as a group called The Chegwins. Their first engagement was at the Floral Pavilion, New Brighton in 1968. Then Keith got himself a spot on the TV show 'Junior Showtime' from the City Varieties Theatre in Leeds. The song he sang was 'What a Wonderful World'. From this, he was asked to appear in a film about twins called 'Egghead's Robot'. Keith took the opportunity to point out that he had a twin brother. Both he and Jeff were hired for the film, which starred Roy Kinnear and Patricia Routledge. It was produced by the Children's Film Foundation. Keith also appeared in another of its productions, 'Robin Hood Junior'.

Both Keith and Jeff were by now boarders at the Barbara Speake Stage School in London. Keith moved to a higher level in Polanski's 1972 film of *Macbeth*, in which he played the part of Fleance, son of Banquo. Jeff acted as his understudy. TV appearances were in 'Black Beauty', 'The Liver Birds' and 'Z Cars', as well as many commercials. Ginger Rogers was the star of 'Mame' in the West End when Keith rehearsed the part of Patrick, but was prevented from appearing by the local education authority. It was felt that his education would be too disrupted. This was only a temporary hitch, for he was allowed to be in the nine-month run of 'The Good Old Bad Old Days' with Anthony Newley and 'Tom Brown's Schooldays'.

At this stage Keith had the idea of suggesting a new children's TV programme to the BBC. It took up the idea. On 8 October 1976, 'Swap Shop' began. It ran for a year, to be followed by the series 'Cheggars Plays Pop'. In 1978 he released his first single record 'I'll Take You Back'. In addition to this, he was involved in game shows and radio programmes. Along the way, he met up with Maggie Philbin, a presenter on the 'Tomorrow's World' TV programme. They were married on 4 September 1983 at the parish church in Maggie's home village, Little Stretton in Leicestershire. They first of all lived in a flat in Twickenham, moving in 1984 to a 17th-century farmhouse in the Hampshire-Berkshire countryside. The future seemed rosy. In fact it was boozy.

The pressures of work were beginning to tell on Keith. His constant activity and travelling began to catch up with him. He started to take refuge in drink. Instead of solving his problems, it created more. By the time he was doing a Sky TV show 'Star Search' five nights a week, he was near collapse. In November 1991 he went into the Priory Clinic, Roehampton for two months of treatment. After coming out, it was not long before he was drinking again. He was back where he started. An abscess, which threatened to burst, necessitated an opera-

*A Cheggers dance routine*

tion at the Princess Margaret Hospital in Swindon. By now Maggie had had enough. With their baby daughter Rose, she moved out of the house. On 4 September 1992 she announced that their marriage was at an end.

After another unsuccessful visit to the clinic, Keith decided to go public. He spoke of his problem on the 'This Morning' programme with Richard Madeley and Judy Finnigan. He also gave an interview about the matter to the *Sunday Mirror*. With great support from Alchoholics Anonymous, the slow path to recovery was commenced. Work gradually came his way once again, with appearances on the ITV children's programme 'Go Getters', as well as Channel 4's 'The Big Breakfast'. He is greatly in demand by all TV companies, including 'Really Annoying Records' on Channel 4 and a documentary on Millennium Babies. In 1999, he compered 'It's A Knockout' on Channel 4, with Frank Bruno as co-host. A nude Cheggers was host of a Channel 5 gameshow 'Naked Jungle' in May 2000. He and his partner Maria live near Newbury in Berkshire. They have a son, Ted, born in 1998.

# Margi Clarke (1955- )

Born in Kirkby, Margi's mother was at one time Mayor. One of a family of 10, Margi came to wider notice when she starred in the 1985 film 'Letter to Brezhnev', written by her brother Frank. She also hit the headlines in her role in 1991 as Ronnie O'Dowd in 'Blond Fist', the story of a Liverpool girl who boxes in New York. Other less notable films were 'All Night Long' and 'Loser Takes All'. She has appeared frequently on TV, including the part of Queenie in the BBC's 'Making Out', and more recently as Jackie Dobbs, a former prisoner, in 'Coronation Street'. She and her family still live in Liverpool.

*Margi Clarke at the Albert Dock, Liverpool*

# Pauline Collins (1939- )

The Collins family lived in Childwall and then New Brighton, where Pauline attended the Maris Stella High School. Her father was a schoolteacher in Liverpool, while her mother taught drama in Toxteth. Grandmother Collins lived at 189 Molyneux Road, Liverpool, where Pauline spent many happy hours. For most of the war years the family lived away from Liverpool. Eventually the local council decided that Pauline's father was not resident in Radnor Drive for long enough periods, even though other members of the family lived there. They all had to move. When her father got a teaching job in Battersea, Pauline attended the Convent of the Sacred Heart school in Hammersmith. The family moved to Worthing in 1959. Like her father, Pauline became a teacher. But acting was her first love. After training at the Central School of Drama and Speech, Pauline's first

work was at a theatre in Killarney. It was here that she had an affair
with one of the actors, Tony. A baby, Louise, was born in the convent
of the Sisters of Nazareth in London in 1962. She was immediately
adopted. It was not until 1986 that Pauline met her again. Although
she appeared with the Windsor Repertory Company and in 'Emergency Ward 10' on TV in 1962, Pauline did not come to public notice
until the 1971 TV series 'Upstairs, Downstairs'. In March 1990 she
was awarded the best actress prize from the British Academy for her
role on the film 'Shirley Valentine'. In 1998-9, she starred as Harriet
Smith in the BBC TV series 'Ambassador'. She is married to John
Alderton, the actor. They have three children, Nic, Kate and Rick.

# Rupert Davies (1916-76)

The award of Pipeman of the Year in 1964 was recognition that
George Simenon's character, Inspector Jules Maigret, had made a
deep impression on the TV public. The role was played by Rupert,
who had been born at 189 Walton Road in a flat over the bank. The
family left Liverpool for South Wales when he was six. During the
Second World War, he was commissioned as an observer in the Fleet
Air Arm. This did not last very long. In 1940, the plane he flew on
minesweeping duties ditched in the North Sea, near the Danish coast.
Captured by the Germans, he spent the rest of the war as a prisoner.

It's an ill wind that blows no good. To provide entertainment in the
camp, Rupert helped to put on shows, ranging from the Marx
Brothers to Ibsen. After the war Rupert made his first official stage appearance while he was understudying Andrew Cruickshank. This
was in the play 'Spring 1600' by Emlyn Williams. A spot in a London
show 'Back Home' by former prisoners of war had preceded this. After a spell in rep, he made his TV debut in 1946. In 1958 he was in the
TV show 'The Army Game'. His career seemed to be made when he
was given the Maigret role in the early 1960s. 52 episodes, involving
18 visits to France for filming, were made in a two-year period. By
then he was the highest paid performer on TV. Such was his stature
that he was named as actor of the year in 1962.

The downside of Rupert's success was that he became typecast. Although he had stage appearances to his credit in *The Merry Wives of
Windsor*, *A Midsummer Night's Dream* and *Henry V*, his career went

*Rupert Davies in his role as Maigret*

into decline. Some rep. at the Old Vic in Bristol, films such as 'The Spy Who Came In From The Cold' and 'Zeppelin', plus a few TV appearances, did not change the position. He was last seen on TV in a lead role in the TV production of Tolstoy's classic *War and Peace*.

After a number of years living in Buckinghamshire, Rupert moved to a 16th-century house on the Lleyn peninsula in Wales. It was here he died from cancer on 22 November 1976.

# Les Dennis (1953- )

Sixteen editions of the TV quiz game 'Family Fortunes' made in two weeks indicate the sort of pressure under which Les works. His father, Leslie Heseltine, was at one time on the books of Liverpool FC, before becoming a bookmaker. His mother was a factory worker. Born on 12 October 1953 at 87 Chesterton Street, Garston, Les was educated at Joseph Williams County Primary and Quarry Bank Comprehensive schools. On Saturday mornings he used to work at Burtons. He subsequently lived at 58 Thornton Road, Childwall and Cromer in Woolton Hill Road.

Les started his career early. After appearing in as many local talent shows as he could, he made his debut at the age of 16 at the Ratepayers Club in Melling. From there, he gradually built up a clientele around the north-western venues. TV exposure came with 'The Comedians' in 1970 followed by 'New Faces', 'The Golden Shot' and

'Crackerjack'. He married Lynne Webster on 1 January 1974. They had a son Philip. After divorce, a second marriage took place, to Amanda Holden on 4 June 1995. In 1976 he was given his TV break in 'Who Do You Do?' He formed a comedy duo with Dustin Gee, appearing in Les and 'Dustin's Laughter Show'. This was brought to a sad end when Dustin died of a heart attack whilst appearing in 'Cinderella' at the Floral Hall, Southport in December 1985.

Back with a solo career, Les became the host of the TV series 'Summertime Special' and appeared in Russ Abbot's 'Madhouse' series in 1986. The following year, he replaced Max Bygraves in 'Family Fortunes', which has continued high in the ratings ever since. On stage, he has had success with 'Me and My Girl' at the Adelphi Theatre in London and in the film 'Intimate Relations'. In 1999 he hosted the TV series 'Give Your Mate A Break'. 2000 saw Les as a star of the West End production of 'Chicago' at the Adelphi Theatre.

# Ken Dodd (1927- )

The keys were thrown onto the stage. The milk-bottles were placed alongside them. It was getting towards midnight. The buses and trains had just stopped running. But Ken Dodd was still in full flow, the jokes still pouring out like machinegun fire. The audience was exhausted, not so much because of the late hour, but because their sides were aching through continuous laughter. This is an experience repeated over and over again by many, like myself, who have sat through a Doddy marathon.

Ken still lives in the same 18th-century detached house at 76 Thomas Lane, Knotty Ash where he was born on 8 November 1927. His grandparents had bought the house when they came from Wales to Liverpool. Grandmother was distinguished by being the city's first lady magistrate. Father was a coal merchant, delivering coal in the surrounding area, as did his elder brother Bill. It was his mother Sara's job to go round collecting the money. She would do this from Thursday to Saturday. One evening, coming back from doing so on the last tram from Prescot, she was robbed of all the money she had collected.

Music ran in the family. Ken's father played the saxophone, once appearing with an orchestra in the village hall in Knotty Ash. In the

1920s he had a short spell as a professional musician. Sara was no mean pianist herself. His father often took Ken to the theatre and music hall, so giving him his great ambition to be on the stage. He put on his own private shows in the backyard of the house, with props made for him by his father. His interest in music was increased by his time as a member of the choir at St John's Church, at which his parents were regular attenders. At Knotty Ash Primary School, he was soon using his talents by presenting Punch and Judy shows. He was eight when he did his ventriloquist act at the St Edward's Orphanage in Knotty Ash one Christmas Day. For his effort he received half a crown. In 1934 he did a show at the school with his dummy, Charlie Brown. He went on to Holt High School, but still entertaining was his main interest. He appeared at venues ranging from the Philharmonic Hall and the Scala, Widnes to the Air Training Corp Cadets in Priory Road, Anfield. At one point he got a job at the Pavilion Theatre in Lodge Lane, helping with the stage props. Unfortunately, on one occasion the house lights went up before he had had a chance to get some of the props off the stage. All this did not mean that he was not interested in educating himself, for he spent a lot of time in the William Brown Library devouring the books of some of the great authors. Not surprisingly P.G. Wodehouse was a favourite.

Leaving school at 14, Ken worked for a while with his father. He drove the coal lorry. All went well until he guided it into a large hole. Then he applied for a reporter's job on the Liverpool Express, but was turned down. He decided it was time to branch out into his own travelling shop business. He sold items such as bleach and firelighters under his own brand, Kaydee Products, around the Dovecot, West Derby and Huyton areas. His speciality was his home-made soap, which had been tried out by his mother first on the floor at home. At the same time, his workload was increasing around the local clubs. He was a member of the Hilda Fallon Road Show, also appearing at the Bradford and Sandon Hotels and St George's, Progress, Hollyoake and Blair Halls. By now Professor Chuckbutty and his famous 'Road To Mandalay' song were part of his act. Each year in the early 1950s he used to put in an appearance at Lavery's sweetshop in Burscough. He was paid in Christmas puddings. One or the other of his jobs had to give. It was Kaydee Products that went.

In 1952 Ken joined Don Ellis's Fairfield Concert Party. Spotted by a producer at The Tivoli in New Brighton, he made his professional debut at the Nottingham Empire in 1954. From this point his career made rapid progress. In March 1955 he made his TV debut in 'The Good Old Days' at the Leeds Palace of Varieties. 1957 saw appearances in 'Six-Five Special' and a summer season in Blackpool. In July 1958, the newspapers announced that Ken was going to get married in September to Anita Boulin, who had been a nurse at Walton and Alder Hey hospitals, but this never came about. The following year his first single record 'Love Is Like A Violin' was released, reaching number two in the charts. His radio series 'It's Great To Be Young' had as one of its scriptwriters a promising young man named Eddie Braben, who lived at 33 Richland Road, Stoneycroft.

Trouble arose at Liverpool University in 1964, when the authorities took a dim view of the students awarding mock degrees in Jam-Butty mining. This was also the year that Ken was made an honorary member of the Cavern in Mathew Street. More practically, Ken's charity work was in evidence in January 1965. He got together with Frankie Vaughan in a bowling competition at the Ambassador Bowl in Wavertree to raise money for the Edge Hill Boys Club. His debut show at the London Palladium, which ran for nine months, took so long that the first house had not ended by the time the second should have started. His shows at the theatre in 1965 and 1967 ran for 42 and 30 weeks respectively. To cap it all, he was invited to take part in the November Royal Variety Show.

Ken's record successes continued too. 'Happiness' was followed by 'Tears', which was at number one for six weeks. These were just two of 19 hit singles. By now he was earning somewhere in the region of £1,000 per week. 1966 was another packed year. He was voted Show Business personality of the year, had a TV series 'Doddy's Music Box' and brought out another hit record 'Promises'. In spite of all this, he probably enjoyed conducting the police band at the Broadgreen Hospital Fête just as much.

There was no shortage of appearances in his home city. His Ken Dodd 'Laughter Spectacular' at the Royal Court in 1971 was a sell-out and his 'Ha, Ha, A Celebration of Laughter' at the Playhouse, two years later, was packed out too. The Royal Court was also the venue for his successful attempt for the Guinness Book of Records on the joke telling record. He managed 1000 jokes in 3 hours 6 minutes, at the same time raising over £1,000 for charity. The Playhouse took its turn as Ken played serious theatre in the role of Malvolio in Shakespeare's *Twelfth Night* in November 1971. When the Queen opened the Queensway Tunnel in June 1971, Ken persuaded Bernard Delfont to hire the Empire Theatre and sell the TV rights for a huge charity concert. To help the Liverpool Anglican Diocese Centenary Appeal in 1980, Ken gave a concert at the Philharmonic Hall. With three bishops present, he started his act by addressing them as 'Bish, bish and bish'. His concern went beyond Liverpool, for in 1975 he helped to save the

*Ken Dodd – 'how tickled I am'*

Palace Theatre in Manchester from being closed by investing £1,000.

A deep sadness invaded the story of happiness. By 1977 Ken had lived with Anita Boulin for 24 years. At the age of 45 she died in Walton Hospital with a tumour of the brain. They had never married because they thought it might have ruined their love for each other. When later he appeared on a BBC programme 'The Psychiatrist's Chair', he admitted that at that point he had lost his faith in God. He described the experience as like knocking on a door and no one answering. That faith was later to return.

The great Diddymen mystery of January 1982 was soon resólved.

One of their number was stolen from Ken's car, which he had parked near the Anglican cathedral. It was quickly recovered in the Sussex Gardens, Toxteth area. The following month Ken was awarded the OBE. This was partly recognition of his work for charity. Amongst other similar involvement, he was patron of the Clatterbridge Hospital Cancer Research Trust, helping to raise over £2 million towards the erection of a research unit. In November 1988 Rotary presented him with the Paul Harris Fellowship Award for his work in aid of cancer. All seemed to be going along smoothly for Ken, but the Inland Revenue had other ideas.

In 1988, it brought charges against Ken Dodd Enterprises. The 27, later reduced to 11, charges were of false accounting going back to 1972. He paid the sum of £825,000 to the Revenue, admitting mistakes but denying criminal intent. The trial was arranged to start on 5 June 1989, but Ken fell ill because of heart problems along with bronchitis. When the proceedings did get under way, the prosecution alleged that he had taken £300,000 over a seven-week period to place in banks in the Isle of Man and Jersey, that he had over £300,000 in banks in Liverpool, plus extra houses in Bankfield Road, Broadgreen and Whitchurch in Shropshire. The grand total amounted to £777,000 in offshore investments and £600,000 in building societies and shares. Witnesses were called, who stated that often the defendant asked for cash or cash as well as a cheque to pay for his appearances.

George Carmen, the flamboyant barrister known as 'Gorgeous George', was the defending counsel. He concentrated of making known how much Ken had done for charity. He pointed out that although he had earned £1 million over 30 years, he did not live in luxury. He added that Ken owned a Jaguar car, which stayed in the garage. The car he used was a Ford Granada. A line of show business celebrities, including Eric Sykes and Roy Hudd, spoke in Ken's defence. His biggest supporter during the trial was Anne Jones, once a Bluebell girl. They had lived together for the past four years, after first meeting at a pantomime at the Alexandra Theatre, Birmingham.

The trial lasted for three weeks. It took the jury 10 hours of deliberation before bringing a not guilty verdict. However, there had been a cost to Ken. The total amount he had to pay to barristers, solicitors and accountants in fees was £44,000, while he reckoned that he lost £100,000 because he had been unable to work for the past months.

Local opinion about the verdict was varied. Some said that there was no chance of Ken being found guilty by a Liverpool jury or if it had been anyone other than him the verdict would have gone against him. Others felt that he was just someone who had made an honest mistake. It was right for him to pay the money owing, but no need for a trial.

Meanwhile, Ken resumed his charity work as well as his stage career. On 3 September 1989 an appearance in Southport raised £9,000. Anne Jones sang in the show, with George Carmen as the special guest. In December he joined in the National Health Service Christmas service at the Anglican Cathedral, reading a lesson. Michael Aspel surprised him with the famous red book in 1990. Ken joked that he thought it was the VAT man. There was a six-week show at the London Palladium 'How Tickled I Am'. The proceeds of one night were given to the NSPCC. He was reported in 1993 as having given £5,000 to enable medical students to gain experience overseas.

Although now at the veteran stage, there is no sign of Ken hanging his tickling stick up. According to him, 'Old comics never die – except in Glasgow'. In spite of his many appearances on radio and TV, he has always been at his best on the stage, with a live audience and no time constraints. Once he appears with his tickling stick and the opening line, 'What a lovely evening for....' then there is no holding him. The hair standing on end and protruding teeth put the audience in a laughing mood straight away. The teeth are a result of falling off his bike as a child. They are now insured for an enormous sum. The only time he has had a hostile reception was when he once canvassed for the Conservative Party in an election in Crosby. Eggs flew in his direction. Like most things that appear easy, Ken puts a great deal of research into his act. He makes a serious study of comedy. At home, there are hundreds of books on the subject. After every performance, the audience reaction is analysed on what he calls his Giggle Map. His boast is that he has never repeated a show. He still makes about 300 appearances a year. He made a late breakthrough into films, appearing as Yorick in *Hamlet* in 1996 and as Mr. Mouse in the 1999 *Alice in Wonderland*.

Ken Dodd is the last exponent of the great British Music Hall tradition.

# Nancy Evans (1915- )

That there was in Liverpool a singer of great talent with a big future became clear at the end of a university lecture by Geoffrey Shaw one day in 1931. Nancy, then 16, sang a setting of Walter de la Mare's poem 'Nod' at the end of the proceedings. Four years later she was well regarded enough to be given a contract with the Purcell club, who were recording the works of the great composer. In the first one she sang the role of Dido in *Dido and Aeneas*.

The daughter of Thomas Evans, a monumental mason of R.O. Evans and Co., Nancy was born on 19 March 1915. From Egerton Road, the family soon moved to 17 Menlove Avenue. Educated at Calder High School, Nancy was then trained by John Tobin, the Liverpool music teacher. She gave her first recital at the Rushworth Hall on 20 March 1933. She made her London debut on 19 March 1934. She gained much success in the 1938 season singing at Glyndebourne, as well as giving a number of recitals in London. On 13 December in that year, she returned to Liverpool to take part in the Liverpool Music Guild Concert in the Bluecoat Concert Hall. The first part was broadcast, which meant Nancy having to sing 11 songs. A critic at the time noted that, 'compared to lesser singers, her contralto voice had no upper layer of thin tone.'

Just before the outbreak of war in 1939, Nancy had taken part in the Covent Garden season, sung opera on the radio and appeared at the Royal Albert Hall. The world of musicals might appear to be a big step from the works of Purcell, but in 1940 Nancy made her debut in 'Rose of Persia'. A run of three weeks might be considered a short one, but her next appearance in 'Top of the World' came to an even more abrupt end after three days. On 7 September the London theatres closed down because of air raid danger. Nancy had more luck with a longer run in 1943 as Natalie in 'The Merry Widow', at Her Majesty's Theatre. In the February she came with the show to the Royal Court in Liverpool.

In August 1944 Nancy joined an ENSA party touring the Middle East, but still found time to be at a concert in the Philharmonic Hall and a midday recital at the Crane Theatre on 10 August. A terrifying moment occurred the following year. In February she undertook a tour of France, Belgium and Holland. At the end of a concert with the

*Nancy Evans: the velvet-voiced contralto*

Hallé Orchestra in Brussels, the audience, as it dispersed, found itself under gunfire from a German plane.

After sharing the title role with Kathleen Ferrier in 'The Rape of Lucretia' in 1946, Nancy went on a continental tour with the opera. In the following years she was in increasing demand. Outstanding performances in this country and on the continent included 'Albert Herring', 'The Beggar's Opera' and 'Love in a Village'. She took part, along with Frankie Vaughan, Arthur Askey and Ted Ray in a radio programme 'Merseyside Merry-go-round' to mark the Liverpool Charter Celebrations in June 1957. In 1968 she played eight parts in 'The Growing Castle' by Malcolm Williamson. She was first married to Walter Legge. They had a daughter Helga born in 1942. In 1949 she married Eric Crozier.

# Kenny Everett (1944-95)

The Cole family should have been in Australia, but instead it finished up in Seaforth. This was because, a few generations previously, a relative had come to Liverpool from Devon to set sail down under. Unfortunately he gambled away his money, so Seaforth was the end of the trail. So it was that Maurice James Christopher Cole was born to Tom, a tugboat skipper, and Lil his wife, a shop worker, at 14 Hereford Road. He had a sister Cathy, two years older. He went to St Edmund's School. He then moved on to St Bede's. At 13 he transferred to a school at Stillington Hall near York with a view to later ordination. Expelled two years later, he returned to St Bede's. Much of early life centred around attending Mass at St Thomas of Canterbury Church, as well as spending time on the sandhills or trips on the overhead railway and Mersey ferry.

*The zany but sad Kenny Everett*

The first job after school was at Cooper's bakery, then at Douglass & Co advertising agency in Chapel Street for four years. Finally, he was advertising manager on the Journal of Commerce and Shipping Telegraph. By now Kenny was producing his own tapes at home. He sent one to the BBC. It was not interested, but Radio London, a pirate station was. He was taken on. The name change to Kenny Everett now took place, taken from the middle name of actor Edward Everett Horton. A highlight for him was being sent to the USA to report the Beatles tour. He was sacked for making inappropriate comments on a programme, as he was by the BBC in 1983 for comments about the wife of the Minister of Transport. His first TV break came with 'Nice Time' in 1968, building up to his most popular show in 1978 'The Kenny Everett Video Show'.

Married first of all to Audrey, a singer, Kenny then married Lee Middleton, whom he met at a Beatles party when he was high on drugs. They married on 2 June 1969 at Kensington Registry Office. On the surface all seemed well – a farmhouse in Cowfold, Sussex, a hill farm in Llandovery, Carmarthen and finally a home in Cherington in the Cotswolds. But Kenny was even more into drugs and Lee had realised he was homosexual. They divorced in 1983. In 1986 Kenny discovered he was HIV positive. His sister came over from Australia to look after him and, two years after he made his condition public, he died in 1995. His funeral took place at the Church of the Immaculate Conception, Farm Street. His ashes were scattered partly in his cottage garden and partly in Dovedale.

# Billy Fury (1940-83)

'The Sound of Fury' stage show still does sufficient business to remind Merseysiders of one of their greatest rock and roll heroes. Ronald Wycherley was the real name of the lad from 35 Haliburton Street. Born on 17 April 1940, his father was a shoe repairer. After St Silas's school, he went to Wellington Road School in Toxteth, where he is mainly remembered for scalding one of the teachers. This happened when he was on tea duty in the staff room. Instead of pouring the tea into a cup, he accidentally directed it onto one of the staff. Long periods of school were missed because of bouts of rheumatic fever. The first, when he was six, resulted in eight weeks in Alder Hey hospital. There was a reoccurrence six years later.

Music was in Billy's blood. Not one for going out much, he spent most evenings at home either practising on the piano and guitar or writing songs. Much of his pocket money went on buying records from Walton's shop in Park Road. Even when he got a job on a Mersey tug with the Alexandra Towing Company, he soon formed a group, consisting of the cook, the mate, the chief engineer and himself. He loved the job, always saying that if his singing career collapsed he would be happy to go back to it. He later worked for a while at Joshua Harris, the wholesalers. Eventually, he sent a tape of his music to Larry Parnes. This gained him a short trial spot on the bill at a show starring Marty Wilde, which Parnes was putting on at the Essoldo, Birkenhead on 1 October 1958. Also in the show that night was a young comedian called Jimmy Tarbuck. Billy, singing 'Maybe Tomorrow' and 'Just Because', was a sensation. Parnes gave him the name Billy Fury, putting him on in his production at Manchester. Then Billy made his first TV appearance, singing one of his own compositions in a play, 'Strictly for Sparrows'.

A record contract with Decca followed. His first record release was in 1959. 'Maybe Tomorrow', backed by the Four Jays, forerunners of the Fourmost, made the top twenty. In November of that year, he appeared at the Empire in a show with Marty Wilde. A planned tour of Ireland with Bridie Gallacher had to be called off. The authorities there came to the conclusion that the way he used the microphone in his act was too suggestive.

1960 saw the release of the album 'Sound of Fury', comprising en-

*Billy Fury – local hero*

tirely his own songs. In March of that year Billy played a week at the Empire. He recalled being very worried that his home-towners would not appreciate him. He need not have worried. Success continued unabated. There was a booking for seven weeks on the ITV programme 'Boy Meets Girl'. There was an appearance in the film 'Play It Cool', directed by Michael Winner in 1962. Two years later, 'I've Gotta Horse' followed. This was about a man going out to buy a dog, but returning with a horse instead. Billy had also literally got a horse. In 1964 he bought Anselmo, which came fourth in the Derby that June. Records continued to flow, including 'Halfway to Paradise' and 'Jealousy'. During these early years of the 1960s, a lot of time was spent on the road, filling theatres up and down the country.

In the middle of the decade Billy's luck began to turn. 1965 was the year of his final hit record 'Give Me Your Hand'. He began to be dogged by ill health. The first sign of decline came when, in January 1966, he had to pull out of a pantomime at the New Theatre in Oxford to rest his voice. There was some good news. On 31 May 1969 Billy married 25-year-old Judith Hall, a fashion model. Their married home was a cottage in Dorking. In 1971 he underwent open-heart surgery, followed by another operation five years later. Worse was to follow. As he waited for a third operation, he was declared bankrupt. By now his marriage had broken down. He retired, along with his girl friend Lisa Rosen, to a farm near Brecon for eight years.

A comeback was being planned. He made two records and appeared on 'The Russell Harty Show' in 1982. Then Billy was taken extremely ill at the farm. He was rushed to a London Hospital. On 28 January 1983 he died. His funeral took place at St John's Wood Church, with burial at Mill Hill Cemetery. A memorial service was held in March at Liverpool Anglican Cathedral. It was conducted by Canon Gordon Bates, with Billy Butler giving the address.

Some saw Billy as the English Elvis. He regarded himself as just a Liverpool lad made good. He was little known abroad, mainly because he got homesick if he was away. Although he had 29 hit records, he never achieved a number one. Nonetheless, he was the outstanding rock and roll singer of his generation.

# Leon Goosens (1897-1988)

Arguably the greatest oboe player of the 20th century, Leon came from an outstandingly musical family. His father Eugene was the conductor of the Carl Rosa Opera Company and his American mother Annie the daughter of an operatic bass singer. His brother Sir Eugene was also a conductor and his sisters, Marie and Sidonie, professional harpists. His brother, the French horn player Adolphe, would have followed in the tradition, if he had not been killed in the First World War.

Eugene and family came to live with his father, who had moved to Liverpool in 1893 to teach voice training after a distinguished musical career. The family lived in a large house in Mount Pleasant, overlooking Brownlow Hill workhouse. Here Leon was born on 12 June 1897. After a short time living in Liscard, the family moved to Chatham Street, opposite to White's Livery Stables. His father was absent most of the year on tour, but whenever the Carl Rosa company appeared at the Shakespeare Theatre, Leon was taken to see the performance. A favourite family outing was to New Brighton Zoo. He was educated at the Christian Brothers Catholic Institute, also attending the Liverpool College of Music for piano and violin lessons. Charles Reynolds, who was principal oboist with the Liverpool Philharmonic Orchestra, gave oboe lessons. Except when it was once stolen and regained, Leon used the same instrument throughout his long career. He was so young when he played in the orchestra under the baton of Sir Thomas Beecham that the great conductor jokingly enquired if he had got a licence. In 1908 he played with his two brothers in the Liverpool Societa Armonica Orchestra in a week of concerts at the Winter Gardens in New Brighton. The family moved to London in 1912.

Between the ages of 11 and 14 Leon studied at the Royal College of Music. Three years later he was principal oboist of the Queen's Hall

Orchestra, under Sir Henry Wood of Promenade Concerts fame. During the First World War he served in the Middlesex Yeomanry and the 8th Royal Fusiliers, eventually gaining a commission in the Sherwood Foresters. He had a very narrow and miraculous escape from death during the Battle of the Somme. An enemy bullet hit a cigarette case in his breast pocket – a present from his brother Eugene. Although not killed, he was sufficiently badly wounded to be invalided out of the forces. Leon decided to take a job on a farm in Argentina. To raise the money for the fare, he gave concerts. So well did he do that he abandoned the plan, deciding to concentrate instead on a musical career. Soon he was back in the Queen's Hall Orchestra. In 1924 he moved on to Covent Garden. At the same time he took up teaching, holding the posts of professor of oboe at the Royal School of Music until 1939 and the Royal Academy of Music until 1934.

Most of the 1920s was taken up with solo work throughout the United States and Europe. When Sir Thomas Beecham founded the London Philharmonic Orchestra in 1932, he immediately asked Leon to be his principal oboist. 1926 was the year of his marriage to Frances Yeatman, by whom he had one daughter. His second marriage to Leslie Burrows took place in 1933. They had two daughters. With the advent of the Second World War, Leon joined the Liverpool Salon Orchestra. Such was his fame by now that contemporary composers such as Sir Edward Elgar and Ralph Vaughan Williams were queuing up to write pieces for him.

Leon was honoured with an OBE in 1950. He was involved in 1962 in a serious car accident, which happened in Sidmonton Road, Brondesbury, North London. He had returned from holiday in Malta for his brother Eugene's funeral on 12 June. Damage to his mouth meant that he was unable to play his beloved instrument. Undeterred, he mastered a new technique. Within four years he was giving concerts once again.

In April 1968 Leon was guest of honour at a concert at the Alexandra Hall, Crosby. It was the occasion of the sixth annual dinner of the Recorded Music Circle. During his visit, he let it be known that he was sad that the Liverpool Philharmonic Orchestra had not invited him to celebrate his 70th birthday the previous year. The hint was taken. The Blue Coat Hall was the venue for a concert by himself and the orchestra in February 1969. The following day he gave a recital at Merchant Taylors' Hall in Crosby. On his 90th birthday a recital was given to celebrate the event at the Wigmore Hall in London.

# John Gregson (1920-1975)

'Genevieve' is the name of the film forever associated with John. Starring along with Kenneth More and Kay Kendall, the story of two cars in the London to Brighton veteran car race, was an unexpected success. A 1954 low-budget film from Pinewood studios, many of the pundits thought it would be a flop. Somehow the story caught the essence of a slice of life that is forever England, even though it was written by an American.

The Gregson family lived at 1 Crawford Avenue, Wavertree. The youngest of three boys and two girls was christened Harold. He attended St Francis Xavier School, leaving at the age of 14. Soon after, his father Ernest, a road surveyor with Liverpool Corporation, died of a heart attack. Because of the need of an income the family moved to a larger house, where mother took in students as lodgers. From school, John joined the Automatic Telephone Manufacturing Company in Edge Lane, moving on to work as a draughtsman for Liverpool Corporation in the Cleansing Department.

Little did John think that, when he was called up in the Second World War, he would literally find himself in deep water. He joined the Royal Navy as an able seaman on a minesweeper. On 6 March 1941, *Kerryado* set sail from the East India Dock in London. It had hardly cleared the Thames Estuary before it hit a mine. The boat began to sink. John found himself in the water with an injured leg. It was an hour before he was hauled out and taken to Newhaven hospital. He was lucky that he was on watch on the deck that night, for all the crew below decks were killed. Although someone told him after the war that he should have been discharged with the injury he had sustained, John remained on the minesweepers, without further mishap, until the end of hostilities.

Just before the war, John had tried, without success, to get an acting job in London. He was more fortunate after the conflict. Soon after demob, the Liverpool Old Vic Company based at the Playhouse Theatre took him on in bit parts. Eight months later, he joined the Perth Repertory Company. It was here he met his wife to be, Thea. At the end of the Perth contract, John returned to Liverpool to face life on the dole. Meanwhile, Thea had gone to London and obtained a job in the open-air plays, organised in Regent's Park by Robert Atkins. She put in a good word for John, who was promised a place in the company for the autumn. It was a long time to wait, so John came to London hoping to find something to see him through the summer months.

In London was a Birkenhead-born casting director, Dorothy Mather, whom John had known from his days at the Playhouse. She got him a role in a play at the Criterion Theatre, called 'A Sleeping Clergyman', starring Robert Donat. Just previous to this, he had played an even more important role when he married Thea at the Sacred Heart Church in Kilburn on 18 June 1946. He had set his heart on getting into the film world. While he was in Perth, he had written to Ealing Studios asking for someone to come and see him in action. The response had been that Perth was a little too far to come. On getting to the Criterion, John wrote again saying that if Perth was too far to go, maybe the Criterion in Piccadilly Circus was a bit nearer. By chance, letters crossed for someone from Ealing Studios had already been to the play. He was so impressed by John's performance that he was asked to audition. The audition led to a small part in the film 'Saraband For Dead Lovers' with Stewart Granger. John had perfected his Scottish accent during his time in Perth. This meant that he was offered a part as a Scotsman. In fact, many people thought he was Scottish and refused to believe that he hailed from Liverpool.

The next step on the film ladder was a role as a petty officer in the highly successful 'Scott of the Antartic'. By now John and Thea had moved from their flat in Kilburn to one in Maida Vale. Thea went back to her home in Nottingham for the birth of their first child Nicholas. The film roles continued to flood in, including 'Whiskey Galore' and 'Value for Money'. 'Battle of the River Plate' in 1956 was premiered on 6 December at the Odeon Cinema, Liverpool. During the day John went back to pay a nostalgic visit to his old school, St Francis Xavier. 'Genevieve' was followed, in 1955, by 'Above The Waves'. Hopes of a Hollywood career were raised when John was asked to go there to audition for a part in 'Miss Sadie Thompson', with Rita Hayworth. They were quickly dashed. He found, on arrival, that the role had already been filled.

By now the family had moved to an expensive house in Mill Hill, a sign that John was reaping financial reward from his career. It continued to flourish. In 1957 he appeared in the Irish comedy 'Rooney' and, in the following year, with Richard Attenborough, in 'Sea of Sand'.

Somehow, in between all his film commitments, John managed to find time for the stage. 'Seagulls over Sorrento' and 'Breaking Point' were among his successes, appearing in the latter at the Royal Court Theatre in February 1963. He then went on to conquer the medium of television with his role of Commander Gideon in the popular series 'Gideon's Way', based on Scotland Yard.

In 1967 John was back near home to open the Southport Flower Show. Then in September he was at the Royal Court Theatre, along with Alistair Sim, in 'Number 10'. The film 'Night of the Generals', also starring Omar Sharif and Tom Courteney, was released in the following year. A visit home in the summer included crowning the Rose Queen at the annual fair at the church of St Anthony of Padua in Childwall. Eamon Andrews opened the famous red book for a 'This Is Your Life' programme in April 1973. Thea and the children, Nicholas, Catherine, John, Sally, Mary and Jimmy were there. Present also were his sister Molly, a Carmelite nun in Reading, brother Ernest, of 36 Alexandra Drive, Aigburth, who had a commercial art business, plus his other sisters – Stella Johnson from Morningside, Crosby and Chris Bird from Limedale Road, Mossley Hill.

On 8 January 1975 John suffered a heart attack and died. In 1968 Paul McCartney had asked him if he remembered a young boy requesting him to autograph his shoe at a pub a decade before. John said, 'Yes, I do. I seem to remember I signed it – I get a kick out of you'. 'Well,' replied Paul, 'it was my shoe.' Perhaps 'I get a kick out of you' is a fitting epitaph from his fans to one of Liverpool's finest actors.

# Deryck Guyler (1914-99)

Frisby Dyke's store in London Road closed in 1935. The building that housed it was destroyed in a 1940 air raid. Six years later the name achieved national fame. In an ad-lib during the ITMA programme, Tommy Handley named a new character in the show 'Frisby Dyke'. The Liverpudlian with the thick Scouse accent was played by Deryck Guyler.

When Deryck was born on 29 April 1914, the family lived at 66 Rullerton Road, off Mill Lane, Wallasey. Within a few months, it had crossed the river to take up residence at 3 Prospect Vale in Fairfield. In 1920 another move was made to a twelve-roomed house at 113

Hartington Road, off Smithdown Road. This is a road, which also played a part in the lives of Rex Harrison, the film star, and Robb Wilton, the comedian, who both lived there at one time. This was home for the next 18 years until the family moved to 13 Aigburth Drive.

The family background was quite a wealthy one. On Deryck's mother Elsie's side was a history of dentistry. Her grandfather, who had a surgery in Rodney Street, is reputed to have been the first to use anaesthetic for teeth extraction. Her father worked in the ship trade. Later, Deryck based a number of his characters on him. His father Samuel owned the firm of Green and Guyler, started in turn by his father before him. He was also a special constable during the First World War. This jewellery shop was at 223 London Road. No one actually knew who Green was, although the story was put about that he was a person who slept on the premises overnight to prevent break-ins. Samuel, by then living at 9 Winchfield Road, Grand Avenue, died in January 1954.

Schooldays were spent first of all at Melrose Preparatory School and then Liverpool College. Here Deryck overlapped for a year with Rex Harrison. He was not the brightest of pupils. After leaving at 16, he spent some time playing in a band made up of his old schoolmates. Here he honed his skills on the drums and washboard. The effectiveness of the latter was added to by frying pans, cymbals and cowbells. He had got the idea when his father took him to see a show at the Empire Theatre at the age of 10. Taken backstage, a member of the band allowed him to try out the washboard. Another of the unusual musical instruments in which he specialised was the Macedonian nose flute, although no others existed, even in Macedonia.

Religion always played a large part in Deryck's life. He felt the call of God to become a clergyman in the Church of England. So he arrived for training at the evangelical Clifton Theological College, Stoke Bishop, Bristol (now part of Trinity College). The next call he received was to leave. After 12 months, the principal felt that God might use Deryck's services elsewhere. In 1945 he converted to Roman Catholicism. The next 12 months were spent in Somerset on a farm belonging to his uncle. Then it was back to Liverpool. Working for his father's firm did not appear an attractive proposition, so he took an office job in shipping. Meanwhile he was also taking speech training with a teacher in Princes Avenue and singing tuition with a musician near Bold Street.

*Deryck Guyler: the first radio Scouser*

This training enabled Deryck to get a job with the Liverpool Rep in 1935. With the outbreak of war, he managed to get his call up put off for six months. He joined ENSA. A play having not done very well, he joined a concert party, where his washboard virtuosity was put to good use. He was called up in 1941. When told that he was to join the police, he thought he was to be on civilian duties. The smile was wiped off his face when he realised that he was to become a RAF policeman. This duty took him no further than RAF Uxbridge. 1941 was also auspicious for being the year he married. On 15 September he wed Margaret McConnell at the Roman Catholic Church of Corpus Christi in Brixton. She was one of a trio called the Lennox Three, whom he had met during his days with ENSA. They later had two children, Christopher, a doctor, and Peter, who became a brother in the De La Salle Teaching Order.

Invalided out of the RAF in 1942 because of eye trouble in the form of a severe squint, Deryck got a job with the BBC, based first in Manchester, then London. His main task was reading the news and appearing in programmes about the war, making over 1500 wartime broadcasts in all. He decided in 1944 that his talents would be better used as a freelance. The following year, he got a role in the St Martin's Theatre production of 'The Shop at Sly Corner'. Then came the call to ITMA. Many people have the impression that Deryck was in ITMA during its wartime run, but in fact his first appearance was not until September 1946.

As Frisby Dyke, Deryck remained with ITMA until the death of Tommy Handley brought it to an end. He suffered such Handley comments as, 'You stand there with a face like the underside of New Brighton Pier at low tide', but it was worth it for the fame it brought him. He told the story of many people sending him souvenirs of Frisby Dyke's shop. One was a shirt label, with the name of the shop on it. He put it in his driving licence for safety. Stopped by a police check sometime later, the policeman looked at the licence and said, 'Thank you, Mr Dyke.'

After ITMA, his career flourished. He was never the star, always a character actor. On radio, he played the lead role in 'Inspector Scott Investigates' for six years. He was in 'Men From The Ministry' with Richard Murdoch, 'Ray's A Laugh', 'Emney Enterprises', 'Just Fancy' with Eric Barker and many other comedy series. Besides taking part in the opening broadcast of the Third Programme, he also took roles in more serious programmes, playing Macduff in *Macbeth* on the Third Programme. Religious broadcasting and Children's Hour regularly called upon him. On TV he was a natural. He was a regular cast member of 'Hugh and I' with Hugh Lloyd, 'Here's Harry' with Harry Worth, 'That's My Boy' with Jimmy Clitheroe, PC Korky in 'Sykes' and the school caretaker, Mr. Potter, in 'Please Sir' with John Alderton.

Deryck's home city was not neglected. In January 1950 he was the narrator on the BBC's 'One City' programme about Liverpool. Later in the year he did the first commentary at the Aintree Grand National over the public address system. Three years later, he introduced a BBC broadcast on the occasion of the university's golden jubilee.

Making model soldiers was Deryck's passionate hobby. A founder member of the British Model Soldier Society, he had over 30,000 models. He also had a huge library of 78s jazz records. He always regarded himself as a comedy actor rather than a comedian. He pioneered the popularity of the Scouse accent in the media, long before the Beatles appeared on the scene. In later years he lived at 180 Norbury Crescent London, before moving to Brisbane in 1992. He died in October 1999.

# Russ Hamilton (1936- )

It's not too often that a broken love affair leads to a hit record, but this is exactly what happened to a young lad from Everton. Ronnie Hulme, from 158 Beacon Lane, had done his national service in the RAF, based at Weeton on the Fylde peninsular. He had been called up, along with his schoolmate Clive Kendall, a budding comedian. During his two years serving the Queen, Ronnie learned to play the guitar. He then worked for seven years with the Metal Box Company. During this time, he had a romance with a girlfriend. She was from Southport – according to the press. He said she was from Blackpool. When she broke off the relationship, Ronnie was distraught. Sitting moping in the canteen one lunchtime, he scribbled a song on the back of an envelope. The first lines were 'When the moon takes the place of the sun in the sky, I'll call for my girlie. We'll go walking by'.

At the time, Ronnie was, in his spare time, a vocalist with a band in Blackpool. Not really knowing what to do with his newly composed songs, he went into the offices of the *Liverpool Evening Express* for advice. He was put in touch with Lonnie Donegan and Frankie Vaughan. Frankie turned down the song 'We Will Make Love' and it took a year to meet Lonnie. Lonnie told Ronnie that he would be willing to look at any songs he wished to send him. By then it was too late. Now working at Butlin's, Ronnie had gone to a small recording studio in London, which he hired for one guinea. In March 1957 he recorded 'We Will Make Love', with 'Rainbow' on the B-side. The recording engineer was so impressed he called in the boss. The boss rushed off to contact a record company. When it heard the tapes, Ronnie was immediately signed up. A change of name was deemed necessary. The director of the record company parked his car in Hamilton Square everyday. So it was that Ronnie Hulme became Russ Hamilton.

In October 1957 Russ appeared on the BBC show 'Off The Record' to receive a golden disc. This recognised the one million sales of the double record. He also won the Songwriters Guild Ivor Novello award as the year's best songwriter. 'We Will Make Love' got to number two in the British charts. 'Rainbow' was a bit hit in the U.S.A., getting to number six. This gave Russ the distinction of being the first British pop star to rate in the American charts. He crossed the Atlantic to spend eight weeks promoting the record on TV programmes such as 'The Big Record', as well as being interviewed by scores of local radio stations. He undertook a nation-wide tour, including a visit to the Liverpool Empire in November. It ended with 10 days of appearances in Copenhagen.

Another double record quickly followed his first success. As with the first, one side 'The Wedding Ring' was popular in Britain and the other 'I Still Belong to You' in the USA. In August 1958 he was back at the Empire Theatre, topping the bill. During the year he toured the USA, Cyprus and Malta. This was the end of Russ's reign in the top flight. Nonetheless, he continued to perform on the club circuit into the 1990s.

# Tommy Handley (1892-1949)

ITMA (It's That Man Again) and Tommy Handley went together like fish and chips. The hit wartime radio programme was remembered

for years afterwards by its catchphrases, 'Can I do you now, sir', 'I don't mind if I do', 'After you, Claud', 'No, after you, Cecil'. If it had not been for the Second World War would Winston Churchill have gone down in history as one of the great Prime Ministers? If it had not been for the Second World War would Tommy Handley have gone down in history as one of the great British comedians? For ITMA first became popular because of the way in which it poked fun at all the committees, rules and regulations spawned by the needs of wartime Britain. It kept a smile on the face of a nation suffering air attacks, bombing and all the deprivations of a beleaguered island.

*Tommy Handley, star of*
*ITMA*

Tommy was born on 17 January 1892 at 13 Threlfall Street in Toxteth. His father, John, was a keeper in days when milking cows were kept in city areas. Mother Sarah was a cleaner. Schooldays were spent at St Michael's School, Aigburth. Tommy appeared in plays both there, at the Aigburth Amateur Dramatic Society and at Toxteth Congregational Church Sunday school, where he was also in the church choir. Further flung concerts were at the Florence Institute in Mill Street and Saturday night penny concerts in Stanley Road.

Leaving school at 14, he was apprenticed to a corn merchant in Brunswick Street. From the office on the second floor, he misspent his time seeing if he could hit the top hats of people passing in the street below with corn seed propelled by a ruler. He was proud to claim that he could hit a hat at 30 paces. Unfortunately for Tommy, one day the man under the hat turned out to be his boss and his commercial career came to an abrupt end. Other jobs included selling prams in a shop in Duke Street and a spell at Riley's, the wholesale stationers. On becoming a commercial traveller, he soon discovered that he could earn more by doing a one-night variety stand than he did in a week on his day job.

During the First World War, Tommy got valuable experience appearing in the concert parties put on to entertain the troops stationed around Merseyside. Sometimes he was on the same bill as the young Arthur Askey. In the summer of 1917 an advert appeared asking for young men to join the chorus of a touring company performing 'Maid of the Mountaihs'. Auditions were held at the Royal Court Theatre and soon Tommy was rehearsing at Daly's Theatre in London. His professional career had started. At the end of the tour, he was called up for service in the Kite Balloon Section of the Royal Naval Air Service. He could not have flown too many balloons, since he spent most of his time giving performances all over the country in the concert party.

After the war, Tommy was soon treading the boards again, first in 'Shanghai', an undistinguished musical at Drury Lane. At the Bedford Palace Music Hall in Bedford, he formed an unsuccessful duo with Jack Hylton, later a well-known bandleader. It was during the next years of touring concert parties, that Tommy developed his most famous sketch 'The Disorderly Room', a satire based on well-known songs of the era. It was written for him by a medical student, Ted Kavanagh, later his writer for ITMA. In these pre-radio and TV days, the same material could be used in an act over and over again. So famous did the sketch become that he was asked to perform it at the 1923 Royal Command Performance before the King and Queen. This happened to be one of the first outside broadcasts made by the BBC from its Savoy Hill studios.

From 1924 Tommy was broadcasting regularly in comedy series. It was during one of them, 'Radio Radiances', that he met his wife, Jean Allistone, herself a star of musical comedies. Exposure on the radio in turn led to many offers of work on the stage.

Although by now living in Egham, Tommy returned often to Liverpool to visit his mother, who was a big influence on his life. It was she who had persuaded him not to turn professional earlier than he did. She lived in Riversdale Road, Aigburth, with her eldest son Jack, a businessman in Manchester. When Tommy once came back for a Liverpool Boys' Club dinner, his mother, aged 84, said a few words to the assembled gathering at the end. Tommy then stood up and said, 'Well, mother, you didn't get many laughs. She's just smoked her first cigar and it's upset her.' She was also present in October 1948, when Princess Margaret attended the 300th edition of ITMA. Since she was deaf, she could not hear a word, so she laughed when the Princess laughed. After listening to the programme at home with the aid of headphones, she would write to her son with comments such as, 'You were good, Tom, but I thought the play which came afterwards was a lot better. I wish you had been an actor.'

In the late 30s Tommy teamed up with Ronald Frankau to perform on radio their very popular 'Murgatroyd and Winterbottom' sketches, which were the precursors of a new brand of quick-fire comedy. In 1939, just before the outbreak of war, he was asked to produce a regular programme 'of nonsense'. So it was the first ITMA was broadcast on 12 July. However, it only became a success with the wartime programmes, the first of which was from the relocated BBC in Bristol. The various series of ITMA moved location as the BBC transferred to Bangor and eventually back to London again. A six-month stage tour in 1940 was not a success, because the mental images of radio did not transfer very well to the stage. The title ITMA was coined by Tommy when he saw a headline in the *Daily Express* referring to Hitler as 'It's that man again'.

The imaginary locations of the show changed over the years. First it was at the Office of Twerps, with Tommy as Minister of Aggravation. Then he became Mayor of Foaming at the Mouth. After periods as manager of a holiday camp and Much Fiddling Manor, finally he was Governor of Tomtopia, a mythical island. The constant flow of memorable characters became national favourites. Funf, the German spy; Mrs Mopp, the cleaner; Colonel Chinstrap, the intoxicated ex-army officer and Ali Oop, who sold saucy postcards. It was only towards the end of the series that Deryck Guyler's Scouse character of Frisby Dyke appeared.

In 1942 Tommy and the cast were asked to perform for the King and Queen at Windsor Castle. He is reputed to have knocked on the door and asked if anyone knew of any good digs. On a visit to do some

*Tommy Handley: that man again . . .*

programmes the same year at the Scapa Flow naval base in the Orkneys, he replaced his own picture on his permit with that of Hitler.

After a sudden haemorrhage on 9 January 1949, Tommy died in a nursing home. His funeral was held at Golders Green crematorium, where fittingly one of the wreaths came from some surviving employees of Frisby Dyke's, the old London-Road shop. For all his admirers it was, in one of Tommy's catch phrases, 'TTFN' 'Ta, Ta For Now'. At a memorial service at St Paul's Cathedral, Dr Wand, the Bishop of London, fittingly said of him, 'The flame of his genius transmuted the copper of our common experience into the gold of exquisite foolery.'

Tommy was remembered as a man who made fun, without spite or malice. Although he disliked criticism, he was generous in the way he made ITMA a team effort rather than a vehicle for his own stardom. A teetotaller, never owning a car, he was undoubtedly a wealthy man. Unfortunately most of his charity work went unheralded. He spent much time helping the National Association of Boys' Clubs. In April 1948, he had brought the ITMA cast to the Philharmonic Hall to perform on behalf of the Liverpool Association of Boys' Clubs. During Salute the Soldier Week, he appeared at the Picton Hall to help an effort organised by the Liverpool Savings Committee. In recognition of his services, the NABC dedicated a memorial swimming pool to his memory at Nash Court, Ludlow.

On 30 January 1949, a memorial service was held at Liverpool Cathedral. It was conducted by Dean Dwelly and the address given by Revd Eric Evans, the Rector of North Meols. The crowd was so great it overflowed into the precincts of the building. In a letter to a local newspaper the day before, fellow Liverpool comedian, Robb Wilton said that whenever he met Tommy in London, he was greeted with the question 'Well, Robb, what's the latest Liverpool one?'

# George Harrison (1943- ) 2oo/

The Beatle who most liked to stay in the background, George was born on 25 February 1943. Home was 12 Arnold Grove, Wavertree. Coming from a family of four, his father Harry was a steward on the White Line cruise ships before going on the buses. Mother Louise was an assistant in a grocery shop. A few years later, the family moved to 25 Upton Road, Speke. After leaving the Liverpool Institute at sixteen, George became an electrician in Blackler's department store in the city centre. His mother bought him a second-hand guitar three years before and he did so well that she later bought him a new one. To pay her back, George did butcher's deliveries on Saturday afternoons.

After playing for a while with the Les Stewart Quartet, George met up with Paul McCartney in 1955. They travelled on the same bus to school. By now, George was in a group called The Rebels. Not long afterwards, Paul persuaded him to join the Quarrymen on 6 February 1958, although another member, John Lennon, was not at all keen on the idea.

Graduating to the Beatles, George was the loner of the group, never close to any of its other members. He was soon fed up with all the travelling involved. The attention of hordes of fans was not to his taste. A solo career appealed to him. In 1968, he produced the soundtrack for the film 'Wonderwall'. The following year his single from the 'Abbey Road' album, 'Something', got to number one in the USA charts. The 1970 single 'Sweet Lord', from the album 'All things Must Pass', was a huge success. The following year, George was chief organiser of a concert in New York to aid the disaster in Bangladesh. More success in 1973 with the album 'Living In The Material World' was followed by a year when anything that could go wrong did. A tour of the USA was a disaster and the album 'Dark Horse' did not get out of the starting gate. To add insult to injury, George split from his wife. After founding Handmade Films in 1978 and taking part in the 1981 memorial concert for John Lennon with Paul McCartney and Ringo Starr, he had a number of fallow years. It was not until 1987 that he got back on track with a British number two, 'Got My Mind Set On You, Sugar'. This, along with the album 'Cloud Nine', repaired his reputation.

George lives with his wife Olivia, at Friar Park, Henley. On 30 December 1999, he was attacked at home by Michael Abram from Huyton.

# Rex Harrison (1908-90)

'Sexy Rexy' was a sobriquet that clung to the lad from Huyton from early days. Four wives and a much-publicised affair that ended in suicide would seem to add truth to the tag. Be that as it may, it would be a pity if it obscured the genius of the greatest film star that Merseyside has produced.

The home of the Harrison family at the birth of Reginald was Derry House in Tarbock Road. There was money on his father William's side of the family. Their previous residence had been the imposing Belle Vale mansion. Bankruptcy meant that this had to be sold. It was demolished, making way for a jam factory, which was not quite of the same architectural standard. Today the area is covered with the houses of the Belle Vale estate in Gateacre.

Father was trained in engineering, but took a post on the Stock Exchange in Liverpool. He was known to have an eye for the ladies, which maybe he passed on to his son. A member of the West Derby hockey club, William won an England cap. He married Edith May Carey. Rex was the third child, Marjorie being born in 1900 and Sylvia in 1904. William died in 1948 and his wife in 1952. Sylvia was later to marry David Maxwell-Fyffe, a barrister and MP who became Home Secretary. At the age of four, Rex started to attend the kindergarten at Huyton College. These were happy days, with summer holidays spent at Penmaenmawr. At the onset of the First World War, the family moved to Sheffield. Here Rex went to Birkdale Preparatory School. It was around this time that he decided to call himself Rex rather than Reginald. On returning to Liverpool, residence was taken up at 5 Lancaster Avenue, near Sefton Park, before a move to nearby 110 Hartington Road.

As a boy, Rex was never in robust health. He was often off school with sickness. Years later it was discovered that he had had tuberculosis, which had later managed to right itself. For the rest of his life he had hypochondriac tendencies, always carrying a supply of pills everywhere he went. His eyesight was also weak. In the early days, he wore a monocle to help this deficiency, cutting quite a figure at places such as the bear garden at the Adelphi Hotel.

In spite of journalists' attempts to say that he was educated at Uppingham, Rex was always proud to insist that he went no further than Liverpool College, where he was a member of Howson's House. Although not an outstanding scholar, he was good at sport, playing in the cricket and rugby teams. His dramatic prowess was soon evident, appearing in the school's performance of *A Midsummer Night's Dream* at the Crane Theatre in Hanover Street. Acting was in his blood, for he was distantly related to Edmund Kean, the great early 19th-century performer. Through a contact of his father's, Rex got an introduction to William Armstrong, the producer at the Liverpool Playhouse, which had been called the Star Theatre until 1917. Armstrong ran the Playhouse from 1922 until 1944, in that time unearthing such talent as Robert Donat and Michael Redgrave, besides Rex himself. Armstrong took him on the staff. His debut was in 'Thirty Minutes in a Street' in 1924. It was not altogether auspicious. He managed to get his one line wrong. Instead of saying, 'It's a baby. Fetch a doctor,' it came out as, 'It's a doctor. Fetch a baby'. Then again, in Eugene O'Neill's play 'The Gold', he had problems. This time it was not his fault. He was made up to play the part of a negro. At one point, he had to climb up and down a palm tree. Unaware that it had been sprayed with a safety chemical, he discovered that his black make-up had turned white. He played the rest of his part with his back to the audience. Armstrong strongly advised him to give up acting.

London called. Rex got a role in a touring version of 'Charley's Aunt'. It was memorable for him, mainly because of one of the long-serving actors in the play. To relieve his boredom, the performer turned his back to the audience. Only Rex could see him catch his false teeth in his hat. The producer was not amused by Rex's howls of laughter.

Three years of treading the boards in theatres up and down the country meant that Rex had a solid grounding in the trade, even though he had not been to drama school. On 26 November 1930 his London debut was at the Everyman Theatre as Hon. Fred Thrippleton in 'Getting George Married'. In 1934 he met and married his first wife, Colette, who was an army major's daughter. Their first child, Noel, was born in January 1935. Put under contract by Alexander Korda, Rex made the breakthrough into films, although he still found time to do stage work. A series of successful films included 'A Storm In A Teacup' (1937) with Vivien Leigh, 'The Citadel' (1938) with Robert Donat and 'Night Train' (1940) with Margaret Lockwood.

By now, the Second World War was well advanced. Rex insisted on being called up in 1942. Because of his eye weakness, he was not fit for active service. Instead he served as a radar officer with the RAF Photographic Reconnaissance Unit, based at Benson in Oxfordshire. His task was to direct bombers back from missions over Europe. He rose in rank from Pilot Officer to Flight Lieutenant. On 25 January 1943 he married his second wife, film star Lilli Palmer, at Caxton Hall Registry Office. A son, Carey, was born on 8 February 1944.

At the end of the war, Rex signed a seven-year contract with 20th Century Fox. His first Hollywood film was 'Anna and The King of Siam'. Scandal was soon to follow. Rex had an affair with Carole Landis, a film actress. The night after he left to do a play in New York, she committed suicide. She dumped many of her personal possessions on the doorstep of Rex's house, but fortunately they were found by a friend and not by Lilli or the press.

By now Rex was wealthy enough to buy a house, St Genesius, in the Italian Riviera fishing village of Portofino. This remained his refuge for many years to come. He entertained a long list of the rich and famous from Greta Garbo to the Duke and Duchess of Windsor. But it was in London that he met the actress, Kay Kendall, one of the stars of 'Genevieve'. An affair began and love blossomed. After the divorce from Lilli, he and Kay were married on 23 June 1957 at the Universalist Church of the Divine Paternity in New York. It was to be a short-lived love story. Before they married, Rex knew that Kay was suffering from terminal leukaemia. She died on 6 September 1959, being buried at St John's, Hampstead.

Lerner and Loewe, after their successes with 'Brigadoon' and 'Paint Your Wagon', were working on a musical of George Bernard Shaw's *Pygmalion*. They persuaded Rex to take the role of Henry Higgins, with Julie Andrews as Eliza Doolittle. Since there was not enough time for him to learn to sing, he learned the distinctive musical speech talk, for which he became famous. While rehearsing, he managed to find time to direct the play 'Nina' at the Royal Court, Liverpool. The leading lady, Edith Evans, had to drop out because of illness. This led to the play being a disaster. From 1957 Rex and Julie did 750 performances of 'My Fair Lady' together. By the time the show closed in New York in September 1962, it had achieved 2717 performances. Then followed a long run in London at the Theatre Royal, Drury Lane. October 22 1964 saw the world premiere of the film 'My Fair Lady', this time with Audrey Hepburn as Rex's leading lady.

During the run of a Chekov play at the Royal Court, Liverpool, Rex met Rachel Roberts. Daughter of a Welsh Baptist minister, she had made her name in 'Saturday Night and Sunday Morning'. He eventually married her on 21 March 1962 at Genoa Town Hall, some 20 miles from Portofino. This relationship lasted until 1971, when Rex married Elizabeth Harris (the former wife of film star Richard Harris) at Long Island, New York.

Professionally, Rex's career continued to prosper with numerous films and stage plays in the USA and Britain. His private life was not so happy. In December 1978 he married Mercia Tinkler. She was 30 years younger than himself, having no connection with acting. In 1980 Rachel Roberts committed suicide. Rex had decided that he would never retire. He received the reward of a knighthood in July 1989 at the age of 81. It was none too soon for he died on 2 July 1990. He was cremated in Manhattan. His ashes were then taken to his beloved Portofino and scattered.

The man, who showed every confidence on stage, was completely uncertain off it. He was often rude and quick-tempered both at the theatre and at home. He always felt the need to be looked after, but found relationships difficult to maintain. Hence his succession of wives. His large ego meant that he was both self-centred and selfish. But it was this very lack of qualities that made him the great actor that he was.

# Michael Holliday (1925-63)

An overdose of tablets cut short the career of the singer with the lopsided grin from Kirkdale. It was a sad end to the life of a talented vocalist. In the late 1950s and early 1960s, he was a well-known face on TV, in addition to having a series of hit records.

There was both sadness and joy in the Miller household at 40 St Agnes Road, Kirkdale when Norman Alexander was born on 25 November 1925. At the same time as his happy arrival in the world, his twin brother was stillborn. His mother, Cissie, was from an Irish background. His father was a seafarer, who originated from New Zealand. This meant that he was away from home for long periods, with Michael and his brothers Bob and Dave seeing little of him. After school at St Alphonsus', Kirkdale, Michael had a series of jobs – delivering milk, helping in a butcher's shop in St John's Market, then a dry-cleaning shop in Moorfields and helping cut-out in a tailor's. Finally he decided to follow in his father's footsteps, joining the Merchant Navy in a ship plying between Liverpool and Africa. With the outbreak of war in 1939, he transferred to the Royal Navy, seeing active service on HMS *Norfolk*. He then reverted back to the Merchant Navy. Dancing one evening at the Grafton Rooms, on leave in Liverpool, he met a girl named Marjorie Lloyd, who lived in Harlow Street, Toxteth. Love blossomed and they were married at Brougham Terrace Registry Office. One day in 1952, he was a member of the crew of the *Queen Mary*, when it docked in New York. Other members of the crew persuaded him to enter a talent contest run by Radio City. He sang 'River Shannon'. To his amazement he found that he had won the $100 prize.

Back home, Michael used his contacts to get a singing job. He managed to obtain a weekly spot with the Eddie Shaw band at Burtonwood US Army camp. It also so happened that his brother Bob ran the catering side of Butlin's at Pwllheli. Bob used his influence to get Michael in as vocalist with the resident Dick Denny band. Apparently Michael was so nervous that it was a few nights before he could pick up the courage to sing. Each year a camp reunion was held at the Royal Albert Hall in London. After Eric Winstone, a well-known bandleader of the time, heard Michael sing at it, in 1953 he offered him a job for three years with his dance band.

From this point, the way was up. An eight-year record contract with Columbia gave Michael a string of hits. They almost did not come about. As he was due to record his first, 'The Yellow Rose of Texas', his brother Bob died. This had such an effect on him that he did not want to go on. But in 1953 he was persuaded that the record would act as a tribute to Bob. This was followed by 'Sixteen Tons' and a number one with 'The Story of My Life'. On 22 July 1955, he made his first appearance on the TV in 'The Centre Show'.

Along with Marjorie and his son, also Michael, Michael moved to live at 'Dailson', a large house in Bishop's Walk, Addington in Surrey. Later the family went on to Burgh Heath near Banstead. In 1957 he had the first of three TV series, 'Relax with Michael Holliday', the stage version of which toured the country. His one and only foray into films was in the 1959 'Life Is A Circus', which starred Shirley Eaton. This gave him the reputation of being a very laid-back sort of person.

In fact, he was the opposite – very shy, a bag of nerves and always under great stress. He did not employ any professional help to make his bookings or manage his financial affairs. The story goes that one evening he heard an announcement on the TV that he was due to appear later on. He had his coat on to dash out of the house before his wife reminded him that the programme was a recording he had made some weeks before.

In addition to his records and TV work, Michael was in constant demand for personal appearances. He was continually travelling around the country, including 20 weeks in Jersey. He did not forget his home city, appearing on the bill at the Empire Theatre in 1958 and 1962. It came as a shock to the whole show business world when his death was announced on 29 October 1963. Because of his laxity about the running of his finances, a lot of money was owed to the Inland Revenue. Faced by this demand, he committed suicide. In a note left for his wife, he wrote, 'By the time you receive this, I trust I shall be in the land of Nod.'

The funeral took place at Anfield Crematorium. His friends rallied around to help. Russ Conway, the pianist, organised a show at the Prince of Wales Theatre in London in January 1964. All the proceeds went to the family. The short career of Michael Holliday was over. Who knows what could have been?

# Rita Hunter (1933- )

Being named after a film might not be seen as an auspicious start to life for someone destined to become a famous opera singer, but that is exactly how Rita Hunter got her Christian name. Father and mother were so shocked to hear that, after 20 years of marriage, a baby was on the way that they decided to celebrate by going to the pictures. The film they went to see was called 'Rio Rita' and so a star was born on 15 August 1933.

The family home was at 27 Limekiln-Lane, Poulton on the Wirral. Rita's father, Charles, had worked as a boilermaker at Cammell Laird's shipyard. He later became a gas fitter and retired in 1956. The family were well-known local entertainers. It was only natural for Rita to follow suit. She appeared in shows at her schools, Poulton Primary and Manor Road Secondary. Out of school hours, she was appearing with the Wallasey Grand Opera Company and the Merrymakers Pantomime Society.

It was very soon apparent that this young soprano, with a range of three octaves, was a star of the future. She went for voice training with Edwin Francis, the leading Liverpool voice teacher, at the same time as another rising Liverpool opera star, Alberto Remedios.

The first foot on the road to fame was secured in 1953 when Rita auditioned at the Royal Court for a job as a principal in the Italian Opera Company, based in Milan. She was acclaimed by the adjudicators as the finest voice they had ever heard in England. In fact, the opera's administrator in England was so impressed that he took her to London for further training at his own expense. Only the second English singer ever to take a principal's role in Milan, Rita began by singing minor parts to gain experience before taking the larger roles. Here she remained for two years.

By 1957 Rita was singing with the Carl Rosa Opera Company, appearing with it at the Royal Court in May of that year, alongside Valerie Griffiths, another Merseysider brought up at 19 Tudor Avenue, Bebington. Singing with a smaller company gave her the chance to gain more experience of performing the larger operatic roles. This was the year that she got married to John Darnley, who was a tenor with the Sadler's Wells Company. She moved on to join this company and the highpoint here was her appearance as Senta in 'The Flying Dutchman' in 1963. She made this role so much her own, that she called her dog Senta. Apparently he only howled when she practised her scales. Also singing at Glyndebourne and with the Welsh National Opera Company, she took Liverpool by storm in 'Cavalleria Rusticana', before a packed house at the Empire.

More success was to come with her acclaimed interpretation of the part of Brunnhilde in Wagner's opera at Sadler's Wells in 1969. It was this role she sang at her debut at the New York Metropolitan Opera in December 1972, receiving a standing ovation.

Large in character, as well as physique, Rita tells the story of an artistic argument with two others, sitting either side of her, at an operatic rehearsal. The other two could not see each other because of Rita's size, so the argument collapsed. Once arriving in England from Australia, a custom's officer asked her to unwrap a suspicious looking object. It turned out to be a didgerydoo. Rita insisted on playing it for him, while he vainly asked her to wrap it up again.

In 1980 Rita was honoured with the award of an OBE, but by now her appearances in Britain were becoming less frequent. This was not by choice, but because she was not being offered work. Although still singing throughout the world, she was most in demand in Australia. So, in 1984, she sold her house in Thames Ditton and, with her husband, made her home over there.

# Glenda Jackson (1936- )

From film star to Member of Parliament and government minister is a career transformation that not too many people make. Glenda has made the change from one form of acting to what some people would consider another very successfully.

Her parents, Harry and Joan Jackson, were living at Joan's mother's house at 161 Market Street, Birkenhead, when Glenda was born on 9 May 1936. The family soon moved from Mrs Pearce's home to a terraced house at 3 Evans Road in Hoylake. Later, another move was made to 21 Lake Place. Glenda's father, who was known as Mick, was a bricklayer, who served in the navy during the war. To make ends meet, her mother did any cleaning or bar jobs that were available. Later the family was added to by younger sisters, Gill, Lynn and Elizabeth. Glenda attended Hoylake Church of England Primary School, first the infants in School Lane, then the juniors in Market Street. She also went to the church Sunday school, where her first recorded stage appearance was saying one line as a shepherd. Next step was to West Kirby Grammar School. This was not the happiest of times for her, leaving school in 1952 with just two 'O' levels. One of the few highspots of that period was going over to Liverpool to see Donald Wolfit in *A Merchant of Venice*. She had, however, started ballet lessons, appearing in pantomime one year at Hoylake YMCA.

A brief spell working in Woolworth's was followed by two years at Boots on the corner of Market Street and Hoyle Road. During this time she attempted to join the local amateur dramatic society, but was turned down. Instead, she joined the YMCA players, making her first appearance in 'Murder at the Vicarage' by Agatha Christie. The leader of the players, Warren Owen, suggested that she ought to take up acting professionally. Passing her audition, she started at the Royal Academy of Dramatic Art in January 1955. After four years here, she

spent a lot of time 'resting' over the next nine years. Her rare employment included spells at Worthing and Crewe reps, plus small parts in
TV's 'Z Cars' and the film 'The Sporting Life'.

At the rep in Crewe, Glenda had met Roy Hodges, 11 years older
than herself. A Warrington man, he was stage manager. He was also
an actor. Whenever he was able to get an acting job, Glenda would follow, getting work as a shop assistant. The couple married at
Marylebone Registrar's Office on 2 August 1958. Then Glenda
achieved a notable first. Appearing in a review at a private club, she
became the first actress to strip on the British stage. Its director, Peter
Brook, must have noticed something more, for he enabled her to get a
three-month contract with the Royal Shakespeare Company in 1964.
In the same year, Roy and Glenda set up home in Blackheath. Son
Daniel was born on 7 March 1969.

Glenda's career went into overdrive when she won a best actress
Oscar for her role in Ken Russell's film 'Women in Love'. The following year she appeared as the divorcee in the film 'Sunday, Bloody
Sunday' and as Elizabeth I in 'Mary, Queen of Scots'. In 1972 she won
an Emmy Award for her title role in the TV production 'Elizabeth R'.
Another Oscar followed in 1974 as best actress in the film 'A Touch of
Class'. Her private life was becoming increasingly fraught. Roy had
been running an art gallery. He sold this in 1974 to start his own theatre company, which turned out to be a disaster. Glenda was rehearsing in London for a tour of Australia, Canada and the USA. Here she
met Andy Phillips, one of the lighting designers. The romance flourished on tour and led to her divorce from Roy in 1976. The new relationship continued until 1982. Glenda did not ignore the stage,
appearing in the West End for six months in the play 'Summit Confer-
ence'. TV viewers will remember her for her guest appearances on the
'Morecambe and Wise Show' in 1971, 1980 and 1982.

Liverpool University bestowed an honorary doctorate in 1978.
Then, in 1983, Glenda opened the theatre named after her in Borough
Road, Birkenhead. Not to be outdone, the then Liverpool Polytechnic
gave her an honorary fellowship. She received this, dressed in robes
designed for her by students of C.F. Mott College.

A Labour Party supporter since her Hoylake days, Glenda kept up
her political interest. In 1973, she had supported a demonstration
held at the Indonesian Embassy, protesting about the lack of rights of
political prisoners. In 1990, she narrated a series on equal rights for

women on BBC TV. It should not have been a surprise when she won
the Hampstead and Highgate seat for Labour at the 1992 general election. In 1997, she became junior minister for environment and transport. Glenda was a candidate in 2000 for the post of Lord Mayor of
London.

# Holly Johnson (1960- )

'Frankie Goes To Hollywood' kept Mersey music on the map in the
mid-80s. The group consisted of Paul Rutherford, Brian Wash, Mark
O'Toole, Peter Gill and the best-known member, Holly Johnson. Born
in February 1960 at 206 Rathbone Lane, off Picton Road, he was christened William John. The family later moved into Penny Lane. The
third child of Eric and Pat Johnson, he had two brothers, John and
James, and a sister Clare. Eric, whose parents ran a sweet shop near
Edge Lane, took much of the responsibility of looking after the children. In addition, he earned the family keep in a series of jobs ranging
from a salesman to a ship's steward. Pat worked at various times for
Meccano and Plessey in Edge Lane, as an Avon lady and at the

Children's Hospital. Other members of the family lived not too far
away, a grandmother in Gladstone
Road and a great grandmother in
the Wavertree area.

Schooldays were spent first at St
Mary's, where Holly also sang in
the church choir, and then onto the
Collegiate School. Out of school
moments were spent either at the
Silver Blades Skating Rink in
Prescot Road, the ABC Cinema in
Old Swan or Edge Lane Boys' Club.
Holidays included outings organ-
ised by the school to the city coun-
cil centre in North Wales,
Colomendy. This always included
the statutory climb of Moel
Fammau, the nearby hill. Family

*Holly Johnson, of 'Frankie Goes To
Hollywood'*

holidays followed the Liverpool trend to Butlin's at Pwllheli. One childhood incident that stuck in his mind was the occasion that Clare, then at St Hilda's School, was chastised by her parents for talking to a coloured boy. The result was that she ran away. She was seen standing at a bus stop and eventually caught hiding in the grounds of the Cenacle, the Catholic Retreat House in Lance Lane.

At the Collegiate, Holly found himself continually goaded by other pupils because they considered him homosexual. With a friend, he immersed himself in music. He spent most of his pocket money on records at Rumbelows or NEMS. They ranged from Georgie Fame to Roxy Music and T Rex. But most of all, he modelled himself on David Bowie, who he went to see at the Empire Theatre in June 1973. He had been a regular Sunday school attender, but his religious beliefs were brought to an end when, at a tent crusade on the Wavertree Mystery, he was told of the Bible's anti-homosexual stance.

With his friend Heath, Holly played truant from school. They would either head for gay pubs like the Lisbon, Bear's Paw, Sadie's Bar Royal and El Masquerade or strum their guitars at home. At other times, he would hang around Newsham Park, observing the goings-on.

By the 80s, Eric's Club, opposite to the Cavern in Mathew Street, was the place where groups got together. Holly spent a lot of time there. Eventually, at the age of 17, he was asked to join the Big in Japan group. A few records were made at Amazon's Studios, which led to the group having releases with the Zoo Company. The group was then transformed into Frankie Goes to Hollywood. The name came about from a newspaper headline, 'Frankie Goes Hollywood'. The word 'to' was added. By now Holly was living at 46 Catherine Street, having moved from Falkner Square. Work started to come in for the group. It played at Pickwick's and Leeds Warehouse, as well as on a BBC Merseyside programme. First sign of the group members' way out approach came at the 'Larks in the Park' show in Sefton Park, where they waved chain saws about.

Walking along Princes Road one day, the words of the song 'Relax' came to Holly. It got good exposure on the ITV programme 'The Tube', which led to a contract for the group with the ZTT record company. From its release in October 1983, the record went to number one in the charts. The video was considered so obscene and some of the lyrics so objectionable by the BBC that it was banned. This only added to the publicity. The group went on a tour of Britain followed by one of Europe. The group's next two records 'Two Tribes' and 'The Power of Love' topped the charts as well, as did its album 'Welcome to the Pleasuredrome' in 1984. Touring now included the USA and Japan.

Decline began to set in. Arguments developed with ZTT and within the group. The 1986 compilation 'Liverpool Album' was a financial disaster. The group split up the following year. After Holly won a long and costly court case against ZTT in February 1988 to win release from his contract, he signed for MCA Records as a solo artist. His album 'Blast' went to number one with singles 'Atomic City', 'Americanos' and 'Love Train' doing well. Then illness started to haunt him. In 1991 this was confirmed as AIDS. He decided, two years later, to make this public through a newspaper. Although he continued to make records such as 'Dreams That Money Can't Buy', the halcyon days were over.

The doctors had told Holly that he would do well to live for two years, but a change of lifestyle and various therapies eventually led to an improvement in health. In recent years he has returned to recording with his own company Pleasuredome. In September 1999 a new single 'Disco Heaven' was issued, followed by the album 'Soulstream' and a re-release of the FGTH hit 'The Power of Love'.

# Hetty King (1883-1972)

One of the great music hall artists, Hetty was a male impressionist at the time that Vesta Tilley and Ella Shields were her great competitors. She was best known for her song 'All the Nice Girls Love a Sailor'. That she was born in New Brighton was due to the fact that her father's touring party 'Will King and His Minstrels' had a show in the town. The King family had rented a house there for the duration of the show. Hetty first appeared on stage at the age of seven. Her first pantomime was at the Royal Court, Liverpool three years later. At the age of nine, she and her father formed a double act. One night at the Bradford Palace she was noticed by an impresario, who gave her a job as principal boy in a Birmingham pantomime.

In 1906 and 1907, she was star billing in shows at the Lyric Theatre, Everton Valley. She made many appearances at the Tivoli in the

Strand. Besides topping the bill at every leading theatre in the country, she toured Australia, New Zealand, South Africa and the USA. In later years, she had a flat, which she shared with her sisters, Olive and Florence, in Leasowe Avenue, Wallasey. She worked right into her 80s, mainly in old time music-hall shows. For example, in 1967 she headed the bill at the Floral Pavilion Theatre, New Brighton. Her death took place in Wimbledon Hospital on 28 September 1972. A trouper to the end, she had done a season in Eastbourne that summer.

# Billy J Kramer (1943- )

What does the 'J' stand for? Some say that John Lennon made the suggestion after the name of his son, Julian. Others say that it does not

stand for anything at all. What is certain is that Billy was born Billy Ashton on 19 August 1943, the youngest of seven. The family lived at 27 Hankey Drive, Bootle. After school, Billy had various jobs, including a diesel fitter for British Rail and a shoe salesman. A possible promotion by British Rail to Crewe was a chance of more money to help the family, but by now his singing career was taking off.

During the evenings he found time to be in the Coasters group and play in the local clubs. When the lead singer left, Billy were persuaded to fill the vacancy. He and his group, the Dakotas, were one of

*Billy J Kramer – No 1 In Bootle*

the bands hired to sing in the clubs of Hamburg at the same time that the Beatles were there in 1960. His first hit record was a Lennon and McCartney song 'Do You Want To Know A Secret?' a number one in 1963. The Beatles pair had not rated the piece very highly. So much so that the tape John Lennon had made of it had ended with the sound of a flushing toilet. This was followed by another number one with

'Bad to Me'. Brian Epstein, his manager, advised against recording 'Little Children', but it still took top spot. Billy had been persuaded to turn professional when Epstein had guaranteed that Billy's parents would be financially looked after. To his eternal regret, Billy had the opportunity to record 'Yesterday', but turned it down. The one he wanted from Lennon and McCartney was 'I Wanna Hold Your Hand', but the pair wisely said it was one the Beatles wanted to record.

By 1964 he was not only in demand up and down Britain, but also in Europe, the USA and Australia. In Australia, he was the unwitting victim of a beating up in his hotel room by a couple of locals who were at an adjoining party. Back home such was his fame by now that the Mayor of Bootle held a reception for him in the Town Hall, although the Mayor let it be known that Billy's was not the sort of music he preferred. A minor scare followed when Billy had his tonsils removed at Park House Clinic, Crosby. Fortunately his voice was not affected. Going solo in January 1967, Billy concentrated on the club circuit, spending much time in the USA. He continues to be in great demand on both sides of the Atlantic.

# Charlie Landsborough (1941- )

The latest of late starters, it was not until 1995 that Charlie made a break through into the big-time country and western scene. He got to number one in the Irish charts with 'What Colour Is The Wind?'. His album sold 300,000 copies.

Charlie was born on 26 October 1941 in Wrexham, where the family had gone to escape the bombing. They returned afterwards to their home in the Birkenhead dock area at 35 Observatory Road, Bidston. One of 11 children, all of Charlie's family, including his father Charles and mother Aggie, were musical. His headmaster blamed his bad school record on 'that damned banjo'. But this did not prevent Charlie becoming a schoolteacher in 1980, on the staff at Portland Primary School in Laird Street, Birkenhead. Previously he had served as a regular soldier in Germany, where he started to play in bands. After buying himself out four years later, he worked for a short while as a postman in Coventry. Almost broke, he went back to Germany. In Dortmund, he joined the Chicago Sect band. During this time he married Thelma, whom he had known from schooldays. Back home, after

*Charlie Landsborough: king of country and western*

a number of jobs, he started teaching. Although he did his best, Charlie was not very keen on it. It earned enough money to enable him to spend the evenings performing in the Birkenhead pubs. Starting at the Northern Star, he then sang at The Pacific for over 20 years.

Leaving teaching to become a full time singer-writer, 1995 saw the success of 'What Colour Is The Wind?' as well as TV appearances and tours all over the UK and Ireland. The following year his album 'With You In Mind' reached number one in Ireland. Charlie recorded an album in Nashville in 1999. He also appeared at the Grand Ole Opry, before an audience of 4000. While there he took part in a service at the Cowboy Church. A very religious man, he once described God as 'the best manager in the world'.

# John Lennon (1940-80)

July 15 1958 was always a day that John remembered with sadness. His mother Julia had called in to see her sister Mimi, with whom John was living at 251 Menlove Avenue, Woolton. As she crossed the road on leaving, she was knocked down and killed by a car. The driver was a learner-driver, who made the mistake of putting his foot on the brake instead of the accelerator. It was during a German air raid that John had been born on 9 October 1940. Julia, who worked as a cinema usherette, had had a difficult married life. She had married Freddie, John's father, after a long courtship, at Mount Pleasant Registry Office. Freddie was then a bus driver, but later went to sea. He lost his job because of trouble he caused on the ship. The marriage also foundered. Julia then married John Dykins, by whom she had three more children.

At three years of age, John had gone to live with his uncle and auntie, George and Mimi Smith at the seven-roomed house in

Menlove Avenue, which was known as 'The Mendips'. George, who died in 1955, was a dairyman by trade. Previous to this, John had lived for a while with his mother at 9 Newcastle Road. This was his grandparents' home, where Julia had sought refuge after the marriage break up. Then she went to live with husband to-be John, known as Bobby, in Blomfield Road, Allerton. Here John used to travel from Menlove Avenue to stay with her during the school holidays.

Moss Pits Lane and Dovedale Primary were John's first schools, before he moved on to Quarry Bank High School. He showed little interest in academic subjects, failing most exams. This was mainly because he had got the skiffle bug. The city was full of Lonny Donegan imitators. John decided that he would add one more to the number. Encouraged by Mimi, who gave him the money to buy a guitar, he formed, with a schoolmate Pete Shotton, a group called the Black Jacks. It soon changed its name to the Quarry Men, after a line in the school song 'Quarry Men, strong before our birth'. On 9 July the group entered a talent show at the Empire Theatre run by Carroll Levis, the TV star maker. He decided that the Quarry Men were not for him.

Church fêtes are two a penny. It was not the sort of event at which John would usually be seen. But he had a reason for being at the one held on 6 July 1957, in the field at the back of St Peter's Church in Church Road, Woolton. After the crowning of the Rose Queen, the fancy dress parade and music by the band of the Cheshire Yeomanry, the Quarrymen had been hired to play in the late afternoon slot. Then they were to perform as a back up to the George Edwards Band at the evening dance in the church hall. One of the group members, Ivan Vaughan, who went to the Liverpool Institute, brought along a school friend of his who was also interested in skiffle. His name was Paul McCartney. He and John immediately hit it off. One link that they had together, besides skiffle, was that of both having lost their mothers. Although they rarely discussed the matter, it was an emotional bond. Paul and John spent hours at Paul's house in Forthlin Road, while some evenings the Quarry Men practised there. After Julia's death, John was devastated. Consequently the group had no bookings for a number of months. By September 1959 the group was playing in the clubs again. Soon its name was to disappear to be replaced, by mid-1960, with that of the Beatles.

It was in November 1966 that John first met Yoko Ono, through an introduction by Paul McCartney. She was a 32-year-old financier's daughter, who worked as a modern artist. Some of her work was on display at an exhibition in London, which John came to see. She had experienced a tempestuous life. Her father had disinherited her because of her first marriage. Her second marriage was to Tony Cox. John, who had being taking drugs regularly for a few years, found that Yoko was on the same wavelength as himself. An affair was soon out in the open. Everyone, including Cynthia, his wife, knew about it. When Cynthia went in May 1968 on holiday with Julian (born 8 April 1963), she came back to find Yoko installed in the house. The marriage was as good as over. Both John and Yoko obtained divorces from their respective partners. They married in March 1969 in Gibraltar. John's attempt to cite Cynthia for her adultery was a little ironic. Part of the honeymoon was spent lying in bed at the Hilton Hotel in Amsterdam. From it, John and Yoko espoused the cause of peace to the media reporters who crowded into the bedroom. This was the start of many such publicity stunts in the name of the peace movement. Back in London, the publicity continued, including a long interview by Eamon Andrews on 'The Eamon Andrews Show'.

The recordings which John and Yoko had made at Kenwood during Cynthia's absence were released as the album 'Unfinished Music No. 1: Two Virgins' a few months after the wedding. The cover excited more interest than the record, featuring nude photographs of the two. To overcome objections, it was sold in a bag. Because he was unable to get a visa for the USA, John and Yoko descended on an unsuspecting Montreal to take to bed once again. It was here that they recorded in 1969, with the newly formed Plastic Ono Band, the 'Give Peace A Chance' hit. The band's first appearance on stage was made at Toronto University. The group consisted of John and Ono, with Eric Clapton on guitar at this stage. Its make-up varied considerably over the years. In December 1969 the band appeared at the Lyceum Ballroom London in a 'Peace For Christmas' concert in aid of UNICEF. A few days later, John and Yoko were making their third visit to Canada. They had a meeting with Prime Minister Trudeau on the subject of – guess what? – peace. The album 'Wedding Cake' was notable for the fact that slices of real wedding cake were issued with it. The theme of peace seemed inseparable from drugs and transcendental meditation. The single 'Cold Turkey' dealt with the former and 'Instant Karma' with the latter. In 1970, an album called 'John Lennon/Plastic

Ono Band' was well received. In the same year the couple gained more publicity by putting on show what were judged to be indecent photos in a London exhibition.

The album 'Imagine' was more in the line of traditional Beatles type music, although it included a few digs aimed at Paul McCartney in 'How Do You Sleep?'. Legal battles with the other former Beatles went hand in hand with the production of a continuous stream of albums and singles. John steadfastly refused a reconciliation with Paul McCartney. In 1973, the other three Beatles came to New York for a meeting to resolve their differences. Although he only lived a short distance from the hotel where the meeting was to take place, John refused to attend. He merely sent a balloon inscribed with the message 'Listen to the balloon'. A few years later, Paul came to his home to try to talk to him. John turned him away.

The last stage appearance of John was at Madison Square Garden in New York. This was to fulfil a promise he had made to Elton John. The two had sung a single 'Whatever Gets You Through The Night' on an album. Elton made John agree that if it got to number one in the charts, he would appear live. And so he did.

In 1975 Sean was born. John then retired to devote himself to domesticity. One last album with Ono was issued – 'Double Fantasy'. On 8 December 1980 John was shot dead by Mark Chapman. On his birthday, 8 October, an oak tree was planted in 1998 in the Strawberry Fields area of Central Park, New York. This was the place that John used to play with Sean.

Always anti-establishment in his views, John was renowned for what were in those days his daring remarks. At the Royal Command Performance in November 1963, he told the audience, 'Those of you in the cheap seats clap. The rest of you just rattle your jewellery.' On receiving his OBE, he remarked, 'It's cheaper than buying one.' The biggest furore came when he said that the Beatles were more popular than Jesus Christ. One radio station in the USA put a ban on playing his records, as well as threatening to burn them. Much as John protested that the quote, from a magazine article published months before, had been taken out of context, it sounded to most people like the sort of remark he would make. John's beautiful song 'Imagine' was first recorded in 1971. It was rereleased in January 2000. His premature death makes it only possible to imagine what the rest of his life may have achieved.

# Gerry Marsden (1942- )

The names of Bill Shankly and Liverpool Football Club are synonymous. Over the Shankly memorial gates in Anfield Road are the words 'You'll Never Walk Alone', the theme song of the supporters on the Kop. Since it became a seated area, the sound has never been the same as in the past. But every time Gerry Marsden, a keen fan, hears the song, it gives him a great thrill. Its composition came about by accident. He had liked the song from 'Carousel' for years, but he thought it was not the sort of thing that anyone would want to record, especially now that the new Merseybeat had flooded the music world. Brian Epstein, Gerry's manager, and the EMI record company took a lot of persuading to market it. When they did, it went to number one in the charts. Played before one of the matches at Anfield, it suddenly caught on with the crowd, and has remained the Liverpool Football Club anthem ever since. Gerry had the privilege of singing it at Bill Shankly's memorial service in Liverpool Anglican Cathedral. The crowning moment for him came when he was asked to perform the song along with 'Ferry 'Cross The Mersey', at the Everton v Liverpool Cup Final in 1989. Although he was on a tour in the Far East at the time, he was flown in for the occasion. As soon as the match was over, he flew back to continue his tour.

Fred and Mary Marsden lived at 8 Menzies Street. Fred worked on the railway, playing a ukulele in his spare time. Mary doubled as a school cleaner and fish and chip shop assistant. Gerry attended Our Lady of Mount Carmel School. He was in the 7th Toxteth Scouts and boxed at the Florence Institute. But music soon became his first interest. With a guitar, bought for him by his father, he formed his own skiffle group. It included Brian O'Hara, who later was with the Fourmost. They played at venues such as the Labour Club in Peel Street, the Florence Institute and Hambledon Hall in Huyton. The group auditioned at the Wyvern Social Club in Seel Street for a tour with Billy Fury, but it was not chosen. Undeterred, Gerry carried on. Hessy's music shop in Whitechapel became a meeting place for many of the group members. Meanwhile Gerry moved from day job to day job. At various times he was on coal deliveries, at the Kardoma Tea Factory in Redcross Street as a chest maker and at Woolworth's in Church Street on van deliveries.

A Mars a day used to help work and play. It did neither for Gerry.

*Gerry Marsden in Matthew Street, Liverpool*

When he tried to change the name of the group to Gerry and the Mars Bars, the firm refused to let the name be used. Then, watching athletics on TV one day, he heard the commentator mention the pacemaker. That was the inspiration for the new and final name of Gerry and the Pacemakers. No longer playing skiffle, Gerry managed to get the group, which included his brother Fred on drums, a lunchtime spot in the jazz dominated Cavern. In 1960 Gerry and the Pacemakers joined the exodus of groups, including the Beatles, to the Hamburg nightclub scene. For a few months they played at the Top Ten and Star Clubs as well as the Kaiserkeller.

Back in Liverpool, Brian Epstein became manager of the group in May 1962, six months after signing up the Beatles. The latter had already broken into the charts with 'Love Me Do'. They were offered 'How Do You Do It?' but preferred to record one of their own compositions. Gerry snapped up the opportunity. In January 1963 the band, comprising Gerry, his brother Fred, Les Maguire and Les Chadwick, made the recording at Abbey Road studios in London. It went to number one, as did 'I Like It' and 'You'll Never Walk Alone' in November 1963. This created a record of three consecutive number one hits. The two following discs 'I'm The One' and 'Don't Let The Sun Catch You Crying' did not keep up the run, although still doing very well.

A row with girl friend Pauline, who came from Hunts Cross, had led to the writing of 'Don't Let The Sun Catch You Crying'. She also figured in the composition of 'Ferry 'Cross The Mersey'. The film of the same title was about to be made. A song was needed. One evening, Gerry and Pauline were driving by the Pier Head. As Gerry saw the ferries, the tune came instantly into his head. If 'You'll Never Walk Alone' had become the personal property of Liverpool Football Club, 'Ferry 'Cross The Mersey' came to belong to the whole of Merseyside. Engaged on 31 December 1964, Gerry and Pauline were married at St Mary's Church in Woolton on 11 October 1965. Their daughter, Yvette Louise, was born in Clatterbridge Hospital on 30 October 1966. Gerry, performing in Newcastle at the time, drove back through the night for the birth. By now the Marsdens were living in Croft Drive East in Caldy. Yvette was baptised at St Agnes RC Church in West Kirby. A sister, Vicky, was born in 1980.

By 1967 it was becoming obvious that the popularity of the group was declining, as record sales decreased. So Gerry decided to go solo. On 1 June he released his first record 'Please Let Them Be'. On 1 February 1968 he replaced Tommy Steele in the musical 'Charley Girl' at the Adelphi Theatre in London. The role was that of an odd-job lad working in a large mansion. Then he had a run of 18 months in 'Pull Both Ends' at the Piccadilly Theatre. But that was the end of theatrical success. The family did not like living in London, so moved back to the Wirral. A new Pacemakers group was formed in 1972. A return was made to the club circuit in this country and overseas tours in Australia, Canada and the USA. Back in England, Gerry and his group toured the theatres playing the songs of the 60s. In 1993, along with Billy J. Kramer and the Searchers, he gave over 70 shows to celebrate the anniversary of his 30 years in show business. For him, the business continues to prosper with a diary full of bookings.

Of all the Merseyside stars, Gerry has been one of the few to remain in the area. This has meant that he has been seen more locally than others. In November 1983 he relaunched the Woodchurch ferry and in December, two years later, was made a Freeman of the Ferry. This was also the year in which he was the focus of 'This Is Your Life'. In July 1991 he performed the unveiling of a plaque memorial to Brian Epstein on the original NEMS shop site.

There was never to be a return to national popularity, but there have been two notable charity efforts undertaken by Gerry. After the

disastrous Bradford City football fire in 1985, Gerry released a new recording of 'You'll Never Walk Alone', which went to number one.
More importantly, nearly £150,000 was raised for the appeal. Four
years later, the Sheffield Hillsborough football disaster was closer to
home in the sense that it involved so many Liverpudlians. 'Ferry
'Cross The Mersey', sung by Gerry, Paul McCartney, Holly Johnson
and the Liverpool Group, the Christians, reached the number one
spot as well.

A large house, plus holiday homes in Spain and Wales, give an in-
dication of a rewarding financial career. There are not many people
who decry this. They are more impressed by his loyalty to the area.

# Billy Matchett (1889-1974)

'Vaudeville' was the aptly named house at 165 Booker Avenue that
Billy lived in for many years, after a spell at 507 Mather Avenue. He
was one of Merseyside's great vaudeville artists, loved in music halls
up and down the country.

A Toxteth lad, he was brought up at 46 Merlin Street. As a young-
ster he belonged to a minstrel group at the Florence Institute. He graduated from there to the Farrar and Griffiths Pierrots at Seaforth.
Semi-professional days started when Billy was engaged to entertain
the customers during the intervals of the silent films at the Park Palace in Mill Street. When appearing at the Westminster Theatre in Liverpool, he was spotted by the manager of the Lyric Theatre, Everton.
He was taken on at the then huge sum of £5 per week. This led on to a
London tour and spots at the Glasgow and Liverpool Empires. Billy
became nationally famous by doing four tours of the countrywide
Moss Empire Theatres. In 1919 Billy married Alice, a Liverpool girl.
They had two daughters, Audrey and Rhona. A son Brian eventually
became general manager of the Bournemouth Symphony Orchestra.

War intervened. Billy served with the King's Liverpool Regiment
on the Western Front. In 1919 he was privileged to bring back the
colours of the old Liverpool Scottish Regiment. A long career in pantomime started in 1920 as Dick Whittington at the Opera House,
Southport. The years up to the Second World War were spent either
in panto or topping the bills at nearly every theatre in the country.
One of Billy's songs, with the catchy title of 'Does Your Chewing Gum

Lose It's Flavour On The Bedpost Overnight?' became a hit. At one stage, he turned down an offer from Chesney Allen to form a double act. What became Flanagan and Allen might have been Matchett and Allen. However, Billy did quite well on his own, touring South Africa with Wee Georgie Wood in 1936 and 1937.

During the Second World War, Billy helped to entertain the troops through ENSA with his 'Matchett's Mirthquakes'. He then worked almost to the end of his life in Old Time Music Hall revivals, usually taking the role of chairman. He died in November 1974 at the Sir Alfred Jones Memorial Hospital in Garston. He was remembered for his great enthusiasm. When he ran overtime in his act, the management was often forced to drag him off the stage with a long hook.

# Paul McCartney (1942- )

Speke Hall, the 16th-century house close to the roar of Liverpool Airport and a 20th-century council house, 20 Forthlin Road, Allerton may not at first glance have much in common. In fact, they do not, except for one thing. They are both owned by the National Trust. In 1995 the Trust bought the former Forthlin Road home of Paul McCartney for £55,000. Refurbished in its original 1950s style, it opened to the public in July 1998.

This was not the first McCartney residence. It was only one of many. Paul was born in Walton Hospital on 18 June 1942. By coincidence, his mother Mary was a nurse on the maternity ward there, but on this occasion was on the receiving end of matters. At the time the family home was 10 Sunbury Road in Anfield. Irish-born Mary had married James from Everton at St Swithin's Church in 1941. The next family move was across the water to 92 Broadway in Wallasey. Then James got a job with Liverpool Corporation. So it was back to living in Liverpool, this time in Sir Thomas White Gardens in Everton. Paul's brother Mike (baptised Peter Michael) saw the light of day on 7 January 1944. By now Mary had returned to nursing, attending to births in the home. Since she was covering the Speke area, a council house was made available at 72 Western Avenue. During his time in Speke, Paul used to enjoy getting out on his bike to explore the surrounding countryside. Favourite places included the ancient village of Hale, with its Mersey shoreline. The final port of call before arriving at

Forthlin Road in 1955 was 12 Ardwick Road. Paul went first of all to Stockton Wood Road School and then, with his brother, was transferred to Joseph Williams Primary on the Belle Vale estate in Gateacre.

Father Jim, who was 42 when Paul was born, had a series of jobs in his working life. As well as working in the Corporation Cleansing department, he had been employed at Napier's Engineering works and by the firm of Hannay Ltd. at the Cotton Exchange. But it was his talent for music that Paul inherited. Jim was an excellent pianist and trumpet player. His 'Jim Mac's Band' was well known in the vicinity some 20 years before. Jim tried to encourage his son's musical talents by buying him a trumpet. Paul soon swapped this for a guitar, because he was excited by the music of Buddy Holly, Bill Haley and Lonnie Donegan that he listened to on Radio Luxembourg.

When he was 11, Paul took and failed the audition for the Liverpool Cathedral Choir. By this time, in 1953, he had won a place at the Liverpool Institute in Mount Street. A fellow traveller was a boy in the year below Paul, named George Harrison. He lived at 25 Upton Green, which was fairly near to the Ardwick Street home of the McCartney family. At school, Paul noticed that one of the desks he used was inscribed with the initials of Arthur Askey, who had passed that way 40 years before.

A pivotal moment in Paul's life was the loss of his mother through breast cancer on 31 October 1956. When he met John Lennon for the first time at Woolton, where the Quarry Men were playing, the two felt a bond together that was more than musical. The fact that both their mothers had died made them feel an unexpressed emotional tie with each other. The two met frequently in the afternoons at Forthlin Road to listen to records, play their guitars and compose. They made their own recordings of their compositions 'Love Me Do' and 'P.S. I Love You'. 50 copies of the former, made by the Quarry Men, were cut. They are now worth in the region of £10,000 each. Much of the time they spent together, they should have been in school or college. Paul also played truant frequently to go to the Playhouse or the Royal Court. It is not surprising that he achieved only one 'A' level and that in English Literature.

Most people expected Paul to marry Jane Asher. He first met her at a concert in the Royal Albert Hall when she was just 17 years old. He then moved into her family home in Wimpole Street. They became

*Paul McCartney: Liverpool music legend*

engaged in December 1967. This was two years after Paul, along with the other Beatles, had received his OBE. However it was not Jane, but an American, Linda Eastman, that Paul eventually married. She was a divorcee with one child. Meanwhile, having found out about an affair that Paul was having with an old flame, Jane Asher had broken off the engagement. Paul and Linda married in 1968. The ceremony took place at Marylebone Registry Office, followed by a service of blessing in the parish church of St John's Wood. A daughter Mary was born on 28 August 1969 to add to Linda's daughter Heather (born 31 December 1963). The family was completed with Stella (born 13 September 1971) and James (born 12 September 1977).

The first solo album that Paul made in 1970 was called simply 'McCartney'. This was more successful than the second 'Ram', even though the latter reached number one in the USA. He went on to form his own band, Wings, which besides Linda and himself, included Denny Laine of the Moody Blues. Linda was not a musician of any great distinction, but Paul wanted her to be with him wherever he went. A furore was caused by the record 'Give Ireland Back to the Irish' in 1972. The following year, the album 'Band on the Run' was recorded in Lagos, because Paul thought that there would be fewer interruptions. In fact, Linda and he got attacked one night on the streets of the city. The consolation was that the album was a hit, but not as big as 'Mull of Kintyre', which Paul co-wrote with Denny Laine. A tour of Japan by Wings was brought to an abrupt halt when Paul was arrested in Tokyo on 16 January 1980 because marijuana had been found in his luggage. Four years previously, he and Linda had been convicted in Barbados on a drug charge. Wings split up soon after this. Paul returned to the number one spot on both sides of the Atlantic with 'Ebony and Ivory', a duet with Stevie Wonder in 1982.

During the seventies and eighties, Paul was involved a number of legal battles. He first of all joined with the other Beatles to sue their lawyer Klein, who they felt was making too much money out of them. When this was settled at some cost, the former members of the group then fought each other for a larger share of the remaining cash. After a decade of dispute, Capital Records agreed in 1989 to pay Paul outstanding royalties of about £50 million. Although he owned the rights to many songs, a lot of his own belonged to ATV music. He had tried to buy the firm out, but the singer Michael Jackson made a higher bid in 1984 to gain ownership. This was surprising because Paul and Michael were good friends, having sung together the previous year on the single 'Say, Say, Say'. A world tour in 1990 was hugely successful, the concert in Rio de Janeiro attracting an audience of 185,000.

Paul's hometown of Liverpool awarded him the Freedom of the City on 28 November 1984. The same day, Liverpool hosted the premiere of Paul's film 'Give My Regards To Broad Street', which was given a bad reception both by the critics and the public. Something completely different was his 'Liverpool Oratorio' performed on 28 June 1991 at the Anglican Cathedral in Liverpool by the Royal Liverpool Philharmonic Orchestra, conducted by Carl Davis. The singers were the massed ranks of the Philharmonic and Cathedral Choirs, with Dame Kiri Te Kanawa as the soloist. The story of Paul's life is covered by the Oratorio. It received mixed reviews. Although it has been performed on a number of occasions since, it has not caught the public imagination to any extent.

By the 1980s Paul's old school, the Liverpool Institute, was empty. Increasingly it was becoming the target of vandals. The joint vision of Paul and Mark Featherstone-Witty to turn the building into the Institute for Performing Arts started in 1989. It was fulfilled on 7 June 1996, when the Queen performed the opening ceremony. The year was crowned for Paul on being made a knight in the New Year's Honours, receiving the honour at Buckingham Palace on 11 March 1997.

The greatest sadness of Paul's life happened in April 1998. Linda died of cancer on their American ranch. She and Paul had never been parted for more than two weeks. Her final appearance in public was at a fashion show put on by her daughter Stella the previous month. Stella's fashion collection shown in Paris for Chloe was a tribute to her mother. Linda was a keen animal lover and vegetarian. After her death Paul continued her crusade, supporting, amongst other things, the Campaign for the Protection of Hunted Animals. He attempted to publicise a poor album of Linda's, released posthumously, by making much of a radio ban on a swear word in one of the songs. Paul returned to play at the reconstructed Cavern on 18 December 1999 to publicise his rock and roll album 'Run Devil Run'.

A close-knit family life was something of which Paul was proud. All the children went to State schools, even though they enjoyed the freedom of large estates on the Mull of Kintyre and later in Sussex. In early 2000, Paul struck up a relationship with Heather Mills, a former model.

# The McGanns

The advice of father Joe to his four sons, Mark, Paul, Joe and Stephen, was clear and simple, 'Be happy and avoid shift work'. He had a tough life. After serving with the Royal Naval Commandos in the Second World War, he spent most of his working life earning money in factories to bring up his family. The Catholic family was very musical, all the boys singing in choirs as children. They made a number of records and appeared together in the musical 'Yakety Yak'. In January 1999 Joe, Mark and Stephen released a single 'A Heartbeat Away', written by Mark, as a commemoration of how much their late father meant to all the family. Their mother, Clare, was a lover of literature, often reading Shakespeare to her family. The only daughter, also Clare, is a TV producer. Acting talents went with the musical. All the brothers appeared in the TV programme 'The Hanging Gale', a story about the Irish Potato Famine.

Paul has had the most notable acting career, studying at RADA, after working with the DSS in Liverpool. After appearing in 'Withnail' with Richard E. Grant in 1986, he starred in Alan Bleasdale's 'The Monocled Mutineer'. He took the role of Dr. Who in an American version of the TV series. In 1998 he played Eugene Wrayburn in the BBC TV series *Our Mutual Friend* by Charles Dickens. Living in Bristol, he has two sons, Joseph and Jake. Joe was a product of the Everyman Youth Theatre, appearing in the TV comedy series 'The Upper Hand', as well as on stage in 'One Fine Day' and the TV drama 'Madame

Bouvary'. Mark first came to notice in 'Lennon' at the Everyman Theatre. He has been involved in many musicals, including 'Guys And Dolls'. His TV career has blossomed, making a big impression in the TV series 'The Grand'. In 1999 he starred in a touring production of *An Inspector Calls* as well as producing a solo album which he also wrote. Stephen, a writer as well as being an actor, wrote some of the scripts for 'The Bill'. He was in the Liverpool comedy series 'Help' in the 1980s. More recently he has played the role of Sean Reynolds in the soap 'Emmerdale'. He is married to Heidi Thomas. They have a son Dominic. Along with Joe, he went on a trek to Peru in 1999 to raise funds for the NSPCC.

# George Melly (1926- )

The arrival of the Beatles and the host of other Mersey Sound groups meant the end of the jazz era in the Cavern. George, along with performers such as the Spinners, had been regulars at the Mathew Street venue. He soon learned to re-invent himself.

The Melly family has a long tradition in Liverpool. Linked to the Holts of shipping fame, his grandfather lived at 90 Chatham Street. He was born on 17 August 1926, the son of Tom and Maud Melly. Tom was a wood broker, while Maud was well known in local amateur dramatic circles. His sister Andrée became an actress. Brother Bill rose to the rank of Commander in the Royal Navy. The family lived at 22 Ivanhoe Road, off Lark Lane. When George was 10, a move was made the short distance to 14 Sandringham Drive. The houses were always full of visiting professional actors known to his mother. After kindergarten in Marmion Road, prep school was an unhappy experience for George. The headmaster of the establishment in Parkfield Road, W.W. Twyne, was something of a martinet. From there, it was to public school at Stowe. Here began the stories of homosexual encounters, exaggerated by the press in later years. As a child, George decided he wanted to be a doctor. With friends, he got in some practice for his proposed future career by dissecting birds and rabbits. He was only 15 when he first appeared on stage in 'The Gay Lord Quex' at the Playhouse.

After leaving school, George served for three years in the Royal Navy from 1944. For two years after this, he worked at the London

Gallery. This helped to increase his love for paintings, which had been gained by seeing those in the homes of the Holt family and visits to the Walker Art Gallery. His lifelong interest was in collecting the works of the Surrealist school of artists, led by Salvador Dali.

From the end of the Forties, George sang with Mick Mulligan's Jazz Band. In 1959 he was voted as the 'Melody Maker's' best male singer of the year. In that year, he was also compere of the BBC 'Bandbox' show. An attempt to enter the pop world with the record 'Run, Come See Jerusalem' was of little effect. When the beat era brought all this to an end, he turned to writing. He was asked to pen a column on pop music for the Observer, going on to be a TV critic for five years. Another three years as a film critic saw him win the 1970 Critic of the Year award. He also wrote numerous articles and books over this period. In partnership with Wally Fawkes, George wrote the Flook cartoons for the Daily Mail, under the joint name of Trog.

His singing gradually began to come back into vogue. He made a long awaited return to the Playhouse in 1972 in 'Come Back George – All is Forgiven'. By 1971 he was singing with John Chilton's Feetwarmers band. They made tours of China, USA and Europe. A highlight of each year was the visit to Ronnie Scott's club in Soho. His atheistic view of life was made evident when he became President of the British Humanist Association from 1972 to 1974. He gained a foothold too on TV by hosting a chat show in 1974. To show solidarity with the miners, he came back to Liverpool in 1984 for a charity show at the Empire Theatre. He had appeared frequently on the Channel 4 'Gallery' programme. In 1990 he compered an art show for children, called 'Painted Tales'.

A first marriage to Victoria Vaughan in 1955 was dissolved seven years later. After another eight years George married again, this time Diana Dawson. He has a son and a stepdaughter. After living for some years in the Portobello Road in London, the family moved to a cottage near Cardigan in Wales. Financed by the sale of some of his drawings, he bought a 13th-century home near Brecon, complete with a length of the River Usk, in 1976. His wellbeing was upset in February 1993, when he was taken ill at the Mercury Theatre, Colchester and treated for a stomach ulcer in hospital. At Christmas 1998, he moved to a house in West London. He continues to appear on stage, radio and TV.

# Ray Moore (1942-88)

'Tomorrow Is Too Late' is the apt title of Ray Moore's autobiography, written in the months before his early death. It describes the ceaseless work and play that brought about a premature demise. Known to millions in the 1980s as the host of the early morning Radio 2 Breakfast Show, Ray was loved by many of his devoted listeners. A hard drinker and smoker, his health finally gave up on him in his prime.

His mother Margaret was born in Bootle in 1914. She was a nurse who worked at Walton and Ormskirk hospitals. In 1940 she met and married 33-year-old Bill Moore, who was a coffin maker. He had had a hard life, losing his mother at the age of two and his father in the First World War. For some years he lived in the Isle of Man with his stepmother, before coming back to Liverpool. He tended to spend a lot of time and money in the Hermitage pub, coming home in a drunken state many a night. Ray's love of drink may have been inherited from him. The family home was a semi-detached house, 2 Cherry Close, reached through Cherry Lane. Ray was born in 1942. Bill and Margaret eventually separated. In 1950 the remaining family went to live in Waterloo.

Ray attended St Luke's Junior School in Crosby. On Sundays, his religious mother made him go to the Scottish Presbyterian Church, plus the Seaman's Mission and Baptist Sunday schools. Ray found a way of escape one Sunday morning. Having been taken ill at church, he was sent to have his appendix removed at Alder Hey Children's hospital in Liverpool. During this period his father came back, having obtained a job at Cammell Laird's shipyard in Birkenhead. Family holidays were spent with some of his father's relatives in the Isle of Man. Ray moved on to Waterloo Grammar School. He wanted to go to university, but his exam results were not good enough. Instead he found himself working on the docks as a cotton sampler. He first did this in the school holidays, findings that the jokes and devious tricks of the dockers were as good an education as he would get at university. He then became a checking clerk with the Docks and Harbour Board. His task was to check the amount of cargo discharged from the ships. It did not take long for him to tire of this. With the help of a few elocution lessons held at Crane's in Hanover Street, he obtained a post as assistant stage manager with Oldham Repertory Company.

During his year there, his one taste of fame was a role in the film 'A Touch of Brass', about the American evangelist Billy Graham.

Through an agent, Ray obtained work in 1962 at a summer show in Sidmouth and more repertory at Swansea. He then wrote to Granada TV in Manchester. Much to his surprise, he got an interview. He found himself as relief announcer at the age of 20. After a short spell with ATV in Birmingham, he returned to Manchester, this time with the BBC. A radio record programme which he hosted was called 'Just A Little Moore'. He was helped to choose the records in the gramophone library by an assistant named Alma Mather. She and Ray hit it off immediately, although Alma was married with a child, David. The marriage was an unhappy one. Soon news of the affair was spreading. Ray gave in his notice. In September 1967 he moved to London. Alma left home to join him. The divorce came through in 1968. The following year Ray and Alma married at Greenwich Registry Office.

Radio 2 was about to begin. Ray managed to get a short contract on the 'Breakfast Special' programme. He also had his own 'Ray Moore's Saturday Night' show, but in 1973 decided that he would do better if he went freelance. After a time of doing bits and pieces, such as voice-overs, he was given his own two-hour show from 5.30am. It was to remain his for years to come. He soon built up a special relationship with his early morning listeners. Letters poured in. People felt that they knew Ray personally, although they had never and would never meet him in the flesh. By now, Ray and Alma were living in a Georgian cottage in Blackheath. The pace was relentless. Ray had to get up at 3.00am every weekday morning. In addition, he was involved in other projects, such as jetting off the Los Angeles to interview Stevie Wonder or doing his programme from a different city each morning in connection with sponsored jogs. The working day was often extending until late in the evening. The strain was beginning to tell.

In the middle of 1987, Ray noticed that there was a small lump under his chin. As the tumour grew and became more painful, he came to the conclusion that it was affecting his ability to continue his radio programme at the high standard he set for himself. In January 1988, he resigned. He also decided that further treatment for his cancer would achieve little. Part of his therapy during these months was the writing of his autobiography. One of his book-signing sessions was at W.H. Smith's in Church Street, Liverpool. Although obviously very ill, he stayed for two hours instead of the one to which he had agreed. During his illness he received great help from a friend in the Salvation Army, Captain Harry Read.

Ray died on 11 January 1989. His funeral took place at All Souls Church in Blackheath. Although Alma had wanted a small, quiet service, the church was packed with his colleagues from the BBC. A memorial service was arranged for 3 March at All Souls, Langham Place, the church opposite to Broadcasting House, London. Broadcast live, it was an uplifting occasion. A practical memorial took place in April 1989, when Alma presented a £40,000 laser machine to Walton Hospital. The London service culminated in the Syd Lawrence Orchestra and the Salvation Army Band playing 'The Best of Times Is Now'. A fitting epitaph for Ray.

# Derek Nimmo (1930-99)

'Oh, golly, gosh' was the catch phrase that epitomised the stammering, effete, upper-class characters that Derek Nimmo portrayed on TV in 'All Gas and Gaiters' and 'Oh Brother', a far cry from the real Derek Nimmo, an actor of long experience and a businessman of no mean expertise.

The family home was at 20 Craigmore Road, Mossley Hill. Derek was born on 19 September 1930, the son of Harry and Marjorie Nimmo. Derek's father, who died in 1960, worked for the State Assurance Company in Dale Street, Liverpool. As a young lad, Derek belonged to the Wolf Cub pack at the parish church. It was while with the cubs that he fell, breaking his nose. The operation to put matters right was not entirely successful, leaving him with the shape of nose which was his distinctive trademark. He attended Booker Avenue Primary School. Here he had his first taste of acting, playing the part of a toadstool in the school's pantomime. Senior school was Quarry Bank High School, where John Lennon was to be a future pupil. Because of the war, family outings were restricted to Otterspool Promenade and the Dingle cast-iron shore.

During these years he went to the Playhouse whenever he could, as well as running dances on a Saturday night at St Barnabas church hall. In his early teens, Derek got in plenty of practice for his future stage career. A story written by him, 'The Little Apple Tree', appeared

*Derek Nimmo, taking a rest from his TV vicar role*

in the Liverpool Echo. He started to do the rounds of any venue that would give him an opportunity to recite 'Albert and the Lion' and other Stanley Holloway monologues. He also offered a ventriloquist spot, with a doll he had been given for a birthday. Wanting to take training in speech and drama, he went potato picking in the school holidays to earn money. With extra financial aid from his father he was able to go to classes. He did well enough to win prizes awarded by the London Academy of Music and Art. He got as far as being offered a part in a London play. But his parents vetoed the plan because they felt he was too young.

Instead, Derek took a job with the Road Transport and General Insurance Company. This was interrupted by National Service in the Signals and Intelligence Corps, which took him to Cyprus and Egypt. On returning in 1952, he joined Goodlass, Wall and Company in Speke, selling paint. One day a young lady named Patricia sold him a ticket for a production by the firm's dramatic society. This not only got him involved again in acting, but also found him a wife. Another member of the dramatic society was his secretary, Audrey Sadler. Recognising his talent, she tried to persuade him to apply for an acting job. When this did not work, she wrote off letters of application on his behalf, forging his signature. The result was that in 1951, he was offered and took a lowly paid job for nine months as assistant stage manager at the Hippodrome in Bolton. He made his debut as Ensign Blades in 'Quality Street'.

For three years after his first stage job, Derek worked round the country. He started off in Worcester as part of Frank Fortescue's Famous Players. One theatre he did not work at was the Liverpool Playhouse, in spite of his many attempts to do so. Jobs were becoming harder to come by. Derek was reduced to selling hot dogs to get some sort of income. Eventually matters began to improve. He found employment at the Winter Gardens in New Brighton, with Patricia working as a waitress in the theatre cafeteria. This led to a role in pantomime in 'Dick Whittington', starring Anne Ziegler and Webster Booth at the King's Theatre, Westminster. Since he was also doing the publicity for the show, he spent time walking the streets with a billboard. He was involved in a tour of 'The Belle of New York' and the run of 'Room for Two', starring Terry-Thomas. During its run he married Patricia at Mossley Hill parish church on 9 April 1955. After a French honeymoon, home for the newly-wed couple was a caravan. They drove around in an old banger of a car, which was constantly breaking down.

Any job was good enough at this stage. Derek managed an Al Martino Britain tour, was producer of a pantomime, starring Alma Cogan at the Chiswick Empire and in charge of a tour with Peter Brough and Archie Andrews. It was during this period that son Timothy was born, to be followed in later years by Amanda, who married George Howard of Castle Howard, chairman of the BBC, and Piers, who became a theatre director. Then Derek was out of work again. There followed spells as a salesman and running a stall in Petticoat Lane, selling bottles of quack medicine. A chance meeting with a producer in Hyde Park led to six months at the Criterion Theatre in 'The Walk of the Toreadors'. Next he was in a play with Vivien Leigh called 'Duel of Angels', which included the Royal Court in its itinerary. While there, Claire Bloom, another of the play's stars, asked Derek to take her round the docks. When its owner saw them wandering around, they were invited aboard one of the ships.

By now the Nimmos were living in Kensington. Derek found himself working in a number of long-running plays, which gave the family increasing security. The run of A.E. Matthews play 'How Say You?' was followed by two years in 'The Amorous Prawn', one year in 'The Irregular Verb of Love' and a period in the musical 'Charlie Girl', with Anna Neagle, at the Adelphi Theatre, London. Then came a six-month holiday in France on the proceeds!

The transition from stage to film took place when Derek had minor parts in 'The Millionairess', starring Sophia Loren, 'The Coast of Skeletons,' filmed in South Africa with Richard Todd and 'Murder Ahoy', starring Margaret Rutherford. When Frank Muir and Dennis Norden, the scriptwriters, noticed Derek's very small TV debut in a play called 'Mr. Justice Duncannon', they gave him a role in Jimmy Edwards' 'The Seven Faces of Jim'. He was so impressive that further work followed with the comedians Terry Scott, Eric Sykes and Stanley Baxter. On radio, he was a member of the Radio Four 'Just A Minute' team for 23 years. Each member of the team had to attempt to speak for a minute without repetition, diversion or hesitation. If he did any of these, he was challenged by the others.

Derek was one of nature's eccentrics. Amongst other things, he reckoned that drinking bats' and lizards' blood was good for the health. So eccentric comedy roles came naturally to him. Ian Carmichael starred in the TV production of P.G. Wodehouse's 'The World of Wooster', with Derek as Bingo Little. Then he was Hon. Freddie Threepwood in 'Blandings Castle'. In 'All Gas and Gaiters', he took the role of the Bishop's Chaplain, Revd Mervyn Noote of St Ogg's Church. The filming of 'Oh Brother' was memorable for Derek, because he trod on a plank, which caused him some damage by hitting him in the face. Filming in Rome in 1969 for the same series, he was dressed in his Brother Dominic garb on the steps of St Peter's. He had his arm round a girl, posing for a tourist photo. A nun reported him to the police, who arrested him. Then followed the series 'Hell's Bells'. In 1971, he was voted Showbusiness Personality of the Year.

By the mid-eighties, Derek had homes both in Lexham Gardens, London and Northamptonshire. Wanting to move into semi-retirement, he began to change track by starting a project he had tested during his National Service in Cyprus. There he had put on plays with a small group of actors. Now, calling the enterprise Intercontinental Entertainments, he extended this by offering to produce plays after dinner in hotels over the world. In between doing this, he and his wife would spend time sailing. These travels are recorded in his 1988 book, the first of many, 'Up Mount Everest Without A Paddle'. In addition, he became an accomplished after-dinner speaker as well as an expert in antique furniture. He was proud to be made a Freeman of the City of London.

Deteriorating health in 1986 led to a heart bypass operation. In December 1998, after falling down the stairs at home, Derek was in a coma at Atkinson Morley Hospital, Wimbledon. He had just returned from producing one of his plays in Kuala Lumpur. He died in Chelsea and Westminster Hospital on 24 February 1999.

# Peter Noone (1947- )

Herman's Hermits were better known in the USA in the mid-sixties than any other British pop group, including the Beatles. Their popularity was high at home as well. Peter's humble home in Chestnut Avenue, Huyton, where he lived with his parents and much younger sisters Suzanne and Louise, was soon to become a focal point for teenage fans. He had had an early taste of fame by being in the TV soap 'Coronation Street'. But it was when he joined forces with Mancunians Karl Green, Keith Hopwood and Barry Whitwam, along with Lek Leckenby from Leeds to form Herman's Hermits that mega-stardom beckoned. A number one came along in 1964 in the shape of 'I'm Into Something Good', followed by 'Silhouettes' and 'Wonderful World'.

To get away from the hordes of fans invading Chestnut Avenue, Peter rented a nine-bedroomed William and Mary-style house, called Beneden Place in Biddenden, Kent in 1967. His parents and sisters went south to join him. Lord Keyes, the owner, thought that he intended to buy the property. He was not pleased when Peter suddenly purchased a hotel in Herne Bay instead. The 10 million records sold across the Atlantic had helped swell the bank balance. Chart hits continued with revivals of old music hall songs such as 'I'm Henry 8th' and 'Mrs. Brown, You've Got A Lovely Daughter'. The group appeared with Stanley Holloway in the film of the latter title, as well as 'The Boys Meet The Girls' and 'Hold On!'.

The 1967 tour of the USA, ending in Honolulu on 8 September, took in 40 cities over a period of two months. In the November, they were off again, this time on a 10-day tour of Mexico and Brazil. Peter decided in 1970 that the time had come to go solo. He left the others to continue as a group, only joining with them again three years later at a reunion held at Madison Square Garden in New York. Deciding to live in California, he undertook TV and other work. As with many others of his era, he is still on the cabaret and club circuit in this country.

# Tom O'Connor (1939- )

Dockers' humour was renowned in Liverpool, where over 20,000 men were employed at the height of its prosperity. Although they had the names they received at baptism, most were re-christened by their mates. For example, there was the Weightlifter (I'll wait here, while you lift that), the Olympic Torch (he never goes out), and the Bald Rabbit (when he gets on a bus he always says 'I've got no fur'). Others included the London Fog (he never lifts), the Vicar (always works Sundays), the Lazy Solicitor (falls asleep on a case) and the Destroyer (always looking for a sub). These are some of the insights that Tom gives in his book 'Take A Funny Turn'. They are based on his experiences with a dad, who was a docker, and a short time working on the docks himself.

The O'Connor story is that of a schoolteacher turned comedian. He was born on 30 October 1939 at 13 Spencer Street, Bootle. His father Pat was a quay foreman at the Gladstone Dock just down the road. There was Irish blood in the family, his widowed grandmother Biddie having married Billy McGrath. His early years were spent during the wartime. With his father away serving in the army, Tom's Uncle Tom became a surrogate father for six years. Tom went to St James' Junior School, where his favourite subjects were English and Maths. A fascination with films meant that he went to the pictures at the Palace or Sun Hall as often as possible, never missing the Saturday morning show at the Gainsborough cinema.

Tom went onto St Mary's College Crosby. A bright lad, keen also on athletics and rugby, he gained sufficient 'A' levels, to go onto Simmaries Teachers Training College at Strawberry Hill in Twickenham.

Because he had passed his exams early, he had to fill in for a year before going to London. For part of the time he helped out at local schools and then worked, with his dad, on the docks. After a while, he spent time with the Liverpool Warehousing Company. At college, he learned the guitar and played drums in a skiffle group. He was also college social secretary, arranging dances and concerts. One ball he organised was at York House in Richmond. Amongst those coming from other colleges was Pat Finan from Keighley in Yorkshire, who was studying at Digby Stuart College in Roehampton. Tom danced with Pat. It was love at first sight. They were married on 28 July 1962 at St Joseph's Church in Keighley, honeymooning at Grange-over-Sands. Tom somehow found time for his athletics, represented Lancashire in the 220 yards low hurdles race at the All England Games held at Belle Vue, Manchester. To make financial ends meet he also did some night work at a bakery and private maths tuition.

The first post for Tom was back home in Bootle, teaching maths at Joan of Arc Junior School. Living at 48 Hornby Road, he found it difficult to support his family on the wage he received. This was made worse when Pat gave up teaching on the birth of their third child. Tom decided that additional income was needed. Money he got for singing in a pub encouraged him to team up with Brendan McCormack as the duo Tom and Brennie. They started off performing for £4 a week, playing country music at The Selwyn pub in Anfield. When Brendan left to pursue a solo career, Tom decided to do an act with more of a comedy element. He was encouraged that his first attempt at the Newtown British Legion club in Wigan went well. This led to many other engagements at venues such as the Embassy Club, Stanley's, Allison's in Litherland and the Montrose and Wooky Hollow clubs in Anfield.

These were exhausting days. Travelling miles, sometimes for an audience of one, he could perform at up to three clubs a night, in addition to his teaching duties during the day. After first giving up teaching in 1965 to go full-time entertaining, Tom found that it did not pay and had to go back to his first career. But this was only a short hold up. Finally, after 12 years as a teacher and reaching the position of deputy-head, he was able to finish for good. By now, he had earned enough money to get a car, so that he could take engagements further afield. In 1971 he was chosen to appear on 'The Comedians', a TV showcase, produced by Johnny Hamp, for up and coming comedians. Others who appeared during the series were Frank Carson and Bernard Manning. But it was Hughie Green, rather than Johnny Hamp, who brought success for Tom. In 1974 Hughie, looking for talent for his TV 'Opportunity Knocks', heard Tom performing at Russells Club. Hughie had spent three days on auditions. He was simply at the club for a meal. So impressed was he, that he put Tom on his November show. Introduced by his school headmaster, Steve Brown, success was immediate. He was the winner on the show for three weeks running and the work came flooding in.

*Tom O'Connor: expert in dockers' humour*

With Billy 'Uke' Scott appointed as his manger, Tom had done a season in the Isle of Man in 1975. Then, the following year, he was asked by Thames TV to host its game show 'Name That Tune'. This led onto participation in similar shows, such as Channel 4's 'Password', 'Gambit', 'The Zodiac Game', 'A Question of Entertainment' and four series of 'I've Got a Secret'. A high spot for him was the Royal Variety Performance in 1976. Two years later, he was involved in 'Cross Wits', which was shown five days a week. No wonder he earned the title 'King of the Game Shows'. Larger earnings meant larger homes. From Bootle, Tom, Pat and the children Stephen, Anne, Frances and Helen, moved to 37 Deangates Lane, Formby. In 1976 they bought 36 Waterloo Road near the golf course in Birkdale. A five-bedroom house in Ascot was purchased later. The Bootle boy was doing well. In the same year, he appeared in the Royal Variety Show and gained the world joke record in 3 hours, 38 minutes, 56 seconds at Park Hall, Charnock Richard. As well as fronting 'Wednesday Night at Eight', 'London Night Out' and 'The Tom O'Connor Road Show', each Christmas he was in pantomime, including Aladdin at the Empire Theatre in 1983. He used his visit to take part in a table-tennis marathon for funds for a lift for the disabled at the theatre.

Known as 'Mr. Clean' among his fellow comedians, Tom had a reputation for never telling jokes involving religion, race or politics. This stemmed mainly from his Catholic upbringing. His grey hair has been with him since his early teens, and his jokes since he started practising them on his school classes. Personal problems, blazoned across the Sunday papers, put an end to his TV and top stage career. In recent years he started performing again on the club circuits and as an after-dinner speaker.

# Beryl Orde (1912-66)

A natural mimic and impressionist, Bootle-born Beryl had won an elocution prize at the Crane Theatre by the time she was six years old. Her stage debut was at the Argyle Theatre, Birkenhead three years later. During the next five years, she toured with Fred Karno, worked in a concert party and was the star of Fol-de-Rols. Her parents, Evan and Gladys, who hailed from Bangor, lived at 52 Alt Road. They had doubts about a career on the stage, but after jobs in biscuit and peanut factories, as well as working as a typist at a decorating firm, Beryl returned to show business at Southend.

Beryl Orde: *mimic of 3000 voices*

She made tours of South Africa, the USA, India and Germany. Then she became known to a wider audience through TV and radio. At one stage she turned down a Hollywood contract for £1,000 per week. She claimed to be able to impersonate over 3000 well known personalities. In 1939 she married Cyril Stapleton, the bandleader. After divorce in 1959, her second marriage in 1954 was to an accountant and estate agent, Ronald Clarkson, the brother in law of Sir Daniel Davies, the royal physician. It was at this time she retired from the stage. She was delighted to become president of Everton Supporters Club. Her favourite home was the 16th-century Pilgrim Cottage at Potterne in Wiltshire. She died in August 1966 at her then home in Fitzjohn's Avenue, Hampstead.

# John Peel (1939- )

A stalwart of Radio 1, John has been with the team of hosts since its inception in 1967. Until recently, his face had not been well known, because he had rarely appeared on TV since he introduced 'Top of the Pops'. Born John Ravenscroft in Heswall on 30 August 1939, most of

*John Peel (right) and friend during a visit back to Merseyside*

his formative years were spent at the family home, Haddon Corner, Nexton Road, Burton, where he lived for 17 years. He was educated at Woodlands School, Deganwy and then at Shrewsbury Public School. His father, Robert, was a cotton importer for Strauss & Co. in Liverpool. On leaving school, John first of all worked as a cotton broker before doing National Service at the Royal Artillery based at Ty-Croes in Anglesey. Then, after a spell at a Rochdale mill, his father suggested that he went to the USA for a year to learn more about the cotton trade.

The year turned into five years and it was not the cotton trade that he learned about. Trading on the American perception that anyone connected with the home town of the Beatles must be good, he got a job on a local radio station KOMA in Oklahoma City. The Americans decided that Ravencroft sounded better than Ravenscroft. He married a 16-year-old American girl, but it was not long before they separated. On his return to Britain in 1967, John decided that radio was more interesting than cotton. He joined the pirate radio station, Radio London, hosting 'The Perfumed Garden' show. His name was changed to Peel, suggested by a typist in the office. It was not long, however, before he transferred to the fledgling Radio One, joining the likes of Pete Murray and Terry Wogan, where his long tenure has included the 'Top Gear' and 'Night Ride' programmes. Over the years, any group or band worthy of the name has done sessions for a Peel programme. Since 1991 he has produced 'Sound City', a Radio 1-programme broadcast from a regional centre over a week every year. In October 1999, it came from Liverpool.

On 31 August 1974, he married Sheila Gihooley. She was taken seriously ill with a brain haemorrhage in 1997, but has since recovered. Home is Peel Acres in the depths of rural Suffolk. There are four children, William, Alexandra, Thomas and Florence. Between them they boast the second names of Shankly, Dalglish and Anfield, giving some idea of their father's allegiance to Liverpool FC. Recently, John has been involved in the Radio 4 programme 'Home Truths' as well as working for radio in Helsinki and Radio Brandenburg in Germany. He has also returned to TV with the Channel 4, 'John Peel's Sound of the Suburbs'. As well as all this, he also provides the voice-over for many programmes.

John was awarded the OBE in 1998. In August 1999, Radio 1 and BBC 2 ran special programmes to celebrate his 60th birthday. On 21 November of the same year, he received an honorary degree from Sheffield Hallam University to add to a previous one from the University of East Anglia.

# Simon Rattle (1955- )

'Baby Rattle' was the nickname given to a young and gifted conductor, when he won the John Player International Conductors Award in Bournemouth in 1974. Simon entered it for fun. With 200 more experienced entrants from across the world, he was thought to have little chance. To his surprise, he won and found himself with a two-year contract as co-conductor of the Bournemouth Symphony Orchestra.

Music was the great love of the Rattle household at 13 Menlove Avenue. Denis Rattle had been a company director, but later trained as an English teacher. But, in addition, he taught recorder, guitar and piano. He had met his wife Pauline in Dover, where she ran a music shop. They married in 1941, soon moving to live in Liverpool. Their first child Susan was born in 1946. The family was completed by the arrival of Simon on 19 January 1955. By the time he was four, Simon was driving the neighbours mad with his drums. Two years later he made his public debut as a percussionist at a concert at the Bluecoat School. Besides taking percussion lessons from John Ward of the Liverpool Philharmonic Orchestra, he also learned to play the piano. At home, he organised Sunday afternoon concerts for the family members.

From his preparatory school, Newborough, Simon went on to Liverpool College. Not being able to play with the Liverpool Schools Orchestra because of school on a Saturday morning, he was allowed early entry into the Merseyside Youth Orchestra, whose conductor was Bill Jenkins. In addition to percussion and piano, he added violin to his studies. In 1966 he won an Education Authority music scholarship, being taught by the 84 year-old Douglas Miller. The following year, he was named Liverpool music student of the year. Giving a piano recital for the Birkenhead Music Society, halfway through one of the pieces he went back to the beginning by mistake.

Not only musical talent but organisational skills were demonstrated by Simon. On 8 May 1970, he volunteered to put on a charity concert at the Liverpool College hall for the local Spastic Fellowship. For it, he both recruited and conducted a 70-piece orchestra in a 2-hour programme before 300 people. His versatility was demonstrated when, on 22 April 1971, he stood in as a piano soloist with the Merseyside Concert Orchestra at the Philharmonic Hall. So many members of the orchestra were ill that the percussion section had to be supplemented with his father on celesta and glockenspiel plus his sister helping out as well. He was also called in when extra percussion was needed for the Royal Philharmonic Orchestra concerts.

Four top grade 'A' levels at the age of 16 were followed, in September 1971, by study at the Royal Academy of Music in London. At the Academy, the respect that other students gave him was shown by his forming an orchestra from their number, called the New London Chamber Orchestra. On 12 May 1973 he made his official debut as conductor of the Merseyside Youth Orchestra at the Philharmonic Hall. The 1974 conductors award cut short his Academy studies. Over the next two years, he conducted almost 200 concerts with the Bournemouth Symphony Orchestra. In 1977 came his appointments as assistant conductor with the BBC Scottish Orchestra and associate conductor of the Royal Liverpool Philharmonic Orchestra. At Liverpool, Simon made his debut with a performance of 'Porgy and Bess' during the Hope Street Festival. When Walter Weller left as principal conductor, it was thought that Simon might be offered the job. Instead, he was appointed conductor of the City of Birmingham Symphony Orchestra, to succeed Louis Frémaux from September 1980. In that month he also married an American soprano, Elise Ross, from whom he was later divorced. A pre-arranged leave to study English literature at St Anne's College, Oxford meant that in the first year in charge of the orchestra he fulfilled few engagements.

However, the next 18 years were a love affair between conductor and orchestra. With help from the local council and Arts Council, there was a major development plan for the future of the orchestra. The new director, Ed Smith, had formerly been with the Liverpool Philharmonic. He and the new conductor formed a formidable alliance. This period not only saw the orchestra moving home to the new Convention Centre in 1991, but also its transformation from a provincial ensemble into one of the world's leading orchestras. From 1991 Simon started a programme recollecting the music of each decade of the 20th century. Living in London, only five months each year were spent in Birmingham. This gave him time to be involved with the London Sinfonietta, the Philharmonia Orchestra and the Glyndebourne Festival Opera. Of all the overseas orchestras that he conducted, he was most at home with the Los Angeles Symphony Orchestra, who on one occasion put a stolen notice on his rostrum which stated 'you must report all noises and rattles on trams or buses'.

In 1986 came the award of the CBE for services to music. By his orchestra, it was known as the 'Chief Birmingham Elephant'. In February of the following year, Simon, conducting the Birmingham Orchestra, made his first visit to the Philharmonic Hall, Liverpool since he left. June 1991 saw him honoured by his home city with an honorary doctorate at the University. A knighthood was bestowed in 1994.

Simon gave his farewell concert with the Birmingham Orchestra in 1998. An expert in Mahler's symphonies and 20th century music, Simon once said 'You have to be 50% lunatic to want to become a conductor'. He was a great supporter of the works of Delius, Sibelius and Richard Strauss. His humility and willingness to learn, plus the vibrancy of his performances, have made him acclaimed throughout the world. He could have had almost any job he wanted, but chose to stay with the City of Birmingham for almost 20 years. His appointment as conductor of the Berlin Philharmonic Orchestra has opened a new and challenging period in his career.

# Ted Ray (1905-77)

Although starting life in Wigan, Ted lived in Liverpool from the age of four. Born on 21 November 1905, he was the son of Charles and Margaret Olden (née Kenyon). It so happened that his father had rented a house there because he had employment as a pub comedian. Ted was given the name of his father, Charles, who had been born in Liverpool. Father was a maker of stained glass, including some of that installed in Liverpool Cathedral.

Charles senior tried and failed to make a living as a comedian, at one time being resident entertainer at the Slip Inn in Manchester. He then became a pub landlord at the Stanley Arms, Chorley and the Bull's Head in

*Ted Ray: first of the stand-up comedians*

Upholland. Ted remembers standing on a beer crate in the bar of the Bull's Head to give his first public performance as a young lad. He also had a less happy memory of falling into nearby Abbey Lakes and having to be rescued. Ted's mother had a serious long-term illness and was taken to hospital in Liverpool. His father sold the Upholland pub, with the intention of buying another one in Liverpool. He found he was unable to do so. He had to get a job as a ship's steward on the *Empress of Britain* instead.

Home was now 28 Apollo Street and later 5 Oakfield Road in

Anfield. The young Ted went to Anfield Road School. The *Liverpool Echo* of the time noted his appearance during the First World War at a charity concert given by the Richmond Baptist church cubs. He also attended the church Sunday school. Remembering his father's advice, 'learn the violin and you will always make a living', he started to take an interest in the violin, being taught by a lady in Lower Breck Road. To pay for the lessons, he earned tips by carrying to Lime Street station the suitcases of passengers who had arrived at the docks. At 11, he won a scholarship to Liverpool College, leaving after three years with a poor academic record, although he did play violin in the school orchestra. His first job was in the office of Silcock's in Great Howard Street.

Ted had visions of becoming a top sportsman. He played as an amateur at outside right for Liverpool reserves, but got no further. To further his aim of riding in the Isle of Man TT races, he bought a motorbike. His mother feared for her son's life. So, when he was not looking, she would puncture the tyres with a knife. After working for a while at the Automatic Telephone and Electric Company in Edge Lane, Ted followed his father as a ship's steward on the American run of the *Samaria*. Arriving back home, he applied for a job in a ship's orchestra and found himself back on the same ship.

Back on dry land, Ted started getting engagements, singing with a band at the Palladium in West Derby Road. He also got jobs playing the violin and singing in between films. He recalls having an orange hurled at him during his spot at a picture house in Scotland Road. His first stage appearance was in 1927 at the Palace Theatre in Prescot, where he called himself Hugh Neek. He met a man called Harry Wardle at a party. They sang a duet together. It was so successful that Wardle got the pair of them an audition with the manager of the Clubmoor Cinema. This led to the formation of the Wardle and Olden duo. Next, going under the name of Nedlo (Olden spelt in reverse), Ted built up an act as a gypsy violinist, appearing first at the Lyric Theatre, Everton Valley.

In 1933 Ted made his London debut at the Music Hall, Shoreditch. It was at this time that Nedlo became Ted Ray, named after a past winner of the American Golf Championship. Ted thought he would keep the surname short to enable his name to be seen more easily on theatre posters. In the same year he met Sybil Stevens, who was a dancer on the bill at the Empire, Birmingham. They married on 11 July at

Croydon Registry Office. Short of a best man, Ted dragged in a passing ice-cream salesman to fill the vacancy. They were to have two sons. Robin was born on 11 September 1934. He made many TV and radio broadcasts, including the BBC2 'Face the Music' and was one of the founders of Classic FM Radio. Married to Susan Stanks, the actress, he died in November 1998. Andrew was born 31 May 1939. He trained as an actor and, as a young man, appeared in the film 'The Mudlark'. He was estranged for many years from his father, who disapproved of his lifestyle. When Andrew said he wanted to leave home, Ted replied, 'I'll help you to pack.'

In the pre-Second World War years, Ted often appeared at the London Palladium as a support act on one of George Black's bills, but it was after the war that his career really took off. He began to make a name for himself on the radio, his first broadcast being from the St George's Hall, Liverpool. In 1949, he started the 10-year radio run of 'Ray's A Laugh', with Kitty Bluett as his wife. For 14 years, he was a panel member of the 'Does The Team Think?' programme. Although he had 'The Ted Ray Show ' on TV in 1955 and appeared in a number of films, including 'Carry On Teacher' in 1959, he was essentially at his best on radio. He toured South Africa three times and appeared on three Royal Command shows. A tireless worker for charity, he was King Water Rat in 1949 and 1950.

The first of the stand-up comedians, who appeared in a suit rather than in costume, Ted Ray had an easy style ideally suited for radio. Typical of his jokes was, 'When I was young the seat of my pants were so shiny that if I'd bent down, I'd have had seven years bad luck.'

Ted died on 8 November 1977. His own summing up of his career was 'From Fiddling to Fooling'. He did it remarkably well.

# Brian Reece (1913-62)

There are not too many police constables around today with a name anything like Archibald Berkeley-Willoughby, but that was the name of the fictional character played by Brian. Those were the days when the police walked the beat alone, with only a wooden truncheon and a whistle for protection. Better known as 'PC 49', the radio series in the 1950s attracted big ratings over the six years it was running.

Born at Three Roods, Regent Road, Noctorum on 24 July 1913, Brian came from a comfortable middle-class family. His father Henry ran both Reece caterers and a dairy started by his father Sam. Henry's offices were in Hawke Street in the Liverpool City centre. His mother, Molly, from Northern Ireland, was known locally as a good singer. Her father, who had been a skilled printer in Belfast, had done some acting. So it was no coincidence that Brian had acting in his blood. Sister Maureen later married Alick Kirk Wilson, the Liverpool surgeon.

Brian's wealthy parents were able to afford a private education for their son. After Somerville Preparatory School, he went to Oakham public school in Rutland. However, he did not shine as a pupil, failing his exams. Back in Liverpool, he found himself under the same cramming tutor as Deryck Guyler.

After joining the Liverpool Rep at the Playhouse in 1931, Brian made his first appearance in the role of a blacksmith in Galsworthy's play 'Strife'. He was also seen at the Winter Gardens, New Brighton and Crane's Theatre in Hanover Street. He suffered a severe bout of peritonitis the following year. The cure involved as much fresh air as possible, so he took a job on a poultry farm in Parkgate for three years. Although the smell was not always to his liking, the breeze from the Dee Estuary did his lungs a power of good. He honed his acting skills during this time by appearing with both the Willaston and Birkenhead Amateur Dramatic societies. With the money he had earned down on the farm, he was able to return to the Playhouse to gain more experience.

By 1938 Brian had moved to London, where he made his debut playing the part of a judge in 'But For the Grace.' He retained his links with the Wirral through his ownership of Hilo Cafe in Parkgate, which was run by his sister-in-law. Brian was called up at the outbreak of war. He soon rose from gunner to officer rank in the Royal Artillery. On 3 June 1940, he married Iris McMaster at the parish church in Neston. Over the years Michael, Christopher and Susan were added to the family. Then, because of health problems, he was transferred to ENSA. He helped to entertain the troops in Italy and in North Africa with the Eighth Army. A highlight was the production of 'The Barretts of Wimpole Street' in the Opera House at Cairo. For two years after that he worked behind the scenes for ENSA.

Back home in Britain, 1947 was a golden year for Brian – the one in which he shot to national fame. Playing in the musical 'Bless the Bride', he began a run of 886 performances in April 1947 at the Adelphi Theatre. This was also the year in which 'The Adventures of PC 49' began on radio. He was also the compere in the 'Starlight Hour' programme. On stage, he next played the role of Count Victor in 'Tough At the Top'. During the Korean War of 1951, he took the Brian Reece show out to the war zone for a month, giving a show a day. Returning to the stage in Liverpool after a break of 20 years, he was in 'What A Man' at the Royal Court. Linking up with a fellow Merseysider, Brian appeared in 'Bet Your Life' with Arthur Askey. He was also in the little man's radio series 'Arthur's Inn' and TV programme 'Before Your Very Eyes'. A short-lived film career came his way in 'Fast and Loose', with Stanley Holloway and Kay Kendall. This followed a run of 'The Seven Year Itch' at the Aldwych Theatre. The workload increased steadily. 1955 was a typically busy year, including TV in 'The Leader Of The House', a Royal Variety Command performance and BBC radio's 'Mixed Blessings'.

A broken leg led to Brian's admission to Westminster Hospital in November 1961. A sufferer from brittle bone disease, his condition gradually deteriorated until his death on 12 April 1962. Five days later his funeral took place at Landican Cemetery on the Wirral.

# Alberto Remedios (1935- )

Can this possibly be the real name of one of the greatest tenors that Liverpool has ever produced? The answer is that Alberto owes his name to a Spanish immigrant grandfather. He was born on 27 February 1935, the son of Albert and Ida, at 166 Grove Street. His parents loved opera, the house resounding to the recorded voices of Caruso and other great singers of the day. Alberto went to school at St Margaret's Primary in Princes Road. His musical education began at the age of seven, when he joined the choir at St Saviour's Parish Church, Falkner Square.

His first job was as an apprentice welder at Cammell Laird's shipyard. He was also a good footballer, playing as a semi-professional for New Brighton, until an injury ended his career. He has remained over the years an enthusiastic supporter of Liverpool FC. But singing was his great love. His voice was trained by Edwin Francis. Coming straight from work one day in his overalls, he arrived at Crane's in Hanover Street for a lesson. He heard a lovely soprano voice coming from one of the rooms. The voice belonged to Rita Hunter and a life-long friendship between the two opera singers began. He gained experience, which would stand him in good stead in the future singing with the Liverpool Grand Opera Company.

At the age of 18, Alberto passed an audition for the Sadler's Wells Opera, which he joined two years later after National Service in the Army. He made his debut as Tinca in 'Tabarro'. In 1958 he won the Queen's prize for the best young opera singer in the country. In April of that year he married Shirley Swindells of 42 Langdale Road at St Bridget's church in Bagot Street. The big career breakthrough came when, just before the first night of a performance of Richard Strauss's 'Ariadne', the leading tenor was taken ill. Alberto was called in to deputise and was a huge success. By 1963 Alberto was married again, to Ava, a soprano from the Sadler's Wells company. A major advance in his career took place in 1965 when he went on tour in Australia on the same bill as Pavorotti. This enabled him to sing alongside such stars of the opera world as Joan Sutherland. In 1968 he sang in Frankfurt, at Sadler's Wells and for the English National Opera.

Alberto sang at the New York Metropolitan Opera for the first time in 1976. The opportunity to sing in Italy gave him invaluable experience of the Wagner operas. He became so proficient that in 1979, when a singer fell ill, he was able to perform the parts both of Siegmund and Siegfried in Wagner's 'The Ring'. A rare feat indeed.

The award of the CBE came in 1981. In latter years, Alberto has lived in Australia. His brother Ramon, (born 9 May 1940) followed in his operatic footsteps. Also a tenor, he trained at the Guildhall School of Music and Drama. At various times, he was a member of the Welsh National Opera Company and a performer at the Cologne Opera House and Covent Garden.

# Anne Robinson (1944- )

Anchorwoman of BBC TV's 'Points of View' and 'Watchdog' programmes, Anne had a solid apprenticeship as a journalist on a number of newspapers. After a job as a shorthand typist, her first experience was with the Fleet Street news agency. She was for a time on the staff of the *Liverpool Echo* and *Daily Mail*. After starting with the *Daily Mail* in 1966, by the age of 23 she was a reporter for the *Sunday Times*, staying for a period of eight years. In 1980 she joined the *Daily Mirror*, within 12 months becoming successively Women's Editor and Assistant Editor. This was followed by spells with *Today*, *The Times*, the *Sun* and the *Express*. Although not giving up newspaper columns entirely, she then moved into radio and TV work in the 1980s. She was a researcher, as well as appearing on the children's show 'Five O'clock Club'. A Saturday morning programme on Radio Two 'The Anne Robinson Show' was notable for some acerbic interviews with Robin Day. 'Points of View', which started in 1987, was a 10-minute, weekly, fast-moving programme, based on viewers' letters about the BBC's output. With a string of different presenters, it has continued down the years. From 1992 'Watchdog' similarly made good use of Anne's journalistic skills, dealing with consumer complaints.

Born on 26 September 1944, Anne's father Bernard was a teacher. The family lived in St Michael's Road, Blundellsands. They were sufficiently well off to be able to spend six weeks of the school summer holidays each year staying at the Carlton Hotel in Cannes. Happy days were spent also on the courts at Hightown tennis club. Anne was sent for speech training to the Shelagh Elliot Clarke school of Dance and Drama in Rodney Street. She got her driving force from her mother, who started with a chicken wholesale business from a cellar at 13 Market Street, underneath St John's Market in Liverpool. This rapidly expanded. Anne thinks that her mother, who died in 1986, sent her to Farnborough Hill Convent College in Hampshire to get rid of her Liverpool accent. This was followed by finishing school at the Ambassadrices in Paris.

Mother made sure that her daughter was not spoiled by getting things too easily. Anne was expected to spend part of each school holiday helping out in the business. This included visits to Stanley Abattoir, where her mother was affectionately known as 'The Duchess'. When she had passed her driving test, Anne made deliveries all round the Liverpool and Wirral areas.

Marriage to Charles Wilson took place in 1968. Daughter Emma was born on 18 July 1970. Three years later the marriage came to an end. She remarried in 1980.

# Robert Robinson (1927- )

'Call My Bluff' was an unlikely TV game requiring celebrities to decide which of the three explanations of an obscure word was true. In the chair was the urbane figure of Robert Robinson. His mother's Liverpool history went back a long way. Her grandmother, Jane Hemming, had married William Jones, who was in the mineral water business. The family of eight children lived in Maria Road before moving to Breeze Hill. Robert's father hailed from Manchester, but had come to Liverpool to work as an accountant for the shipping business of Paul and Preston. He later moved to United Africa Company. Robert's relatives were spread round the city, with his Aunt Marie having a sweet shop and post office on the corner of Stanley Park Avenue.

When the United Africa Company amalgamated with the Niger Company, many jobs were lost. Robert's father was moved to London by the firm, where the family had a home in the Raynes Park area. Robert took a degree at Exeter College, Oxford. He returned to Liverpool to stay with relatives during the war, working for a branch of his father's old company. He later went into journalism, working for the *Sunday Times, The Observer* and the *Sunday Telegraph*. In addition to 'Call my Bluff', he has been also a leading light in 'Points of View', 'Stop The Week' and 'Brain of Britain'.

# Norman Rossington (1928-99)

'A mug like a jug' was Norman's own description of his greatest asset. Instantly recognisable, he played supporting roles in hundreds of film, play and TV roles. Like Deryck Guyler, he was never at the top of the bill. He once said, 'I don't want to be recognised in the street and asked for my autograph. It's more important to me to be recognised in my profession.'

Norman was born at the Railway Inn, 78 Wellington Road, Wavertree on 24 December 1928 – an early Christmas present for his parents. They ran the pub until it was bombed. The family evacuated to Southport. Back in Liverpool, Norman went to Sefton Park School. Leaving at 14, he went to work on the docks. Here he graduated from running messages to being an apprentice joiner. In the evenings he attended the Technical College. This enabled him to move into a drawing office as a draughtsman. He seemed well set for a future career. But acting was in his blood. One evening he did a sketch with a friend at a church social. The friend was Kenneth Cope, who also later pursued an acting career, appearing in later life in series such as 'Randall And Hopkirk (Deceased)'.

Soon after joining a local drama group, Norman's acting ability was recognised. After starting at the David Lewis Theatre, he went to drama school in London at the age of 18. From joining the New Theatre Company, he went to Bristol to train at the Old Vic. He then joined the company at the Bristol Theatre Royal. A period of years followed in the 1950s during which work was hard to come by. He kept body and soul together by working as a chef in police canteens.

The turning point for Norman came in 1957 when he was offered the part of Private Cook, nicknamed Cupcake, in the TV series 'The Army Game'. From this point on, he was always in demand. The following year he appeared in the film 'Carry On Sergeant', to be followed by two others in the Carry On series. In 1964 he took the role of the Beatles manager in 'A Hard Day's Night'. He moved on to Hollywood three years later to appear with Rock Hudson in 'Tobruk' and Elvis Presley in 'Double Trouble'. Other film credits were in 'A Night To Remember', 'The Longest Day', 'Lawrence of Arabia', 'Those Magnificent Men In Their Flying Machines' and 'The Charge Of The Light Brigade'.

In the 70s most of Norman's work was on TV, although in 1991 he was in a film about Derek Bentley called 'Let Him Have It'. The roles were not always comic ones. For instance in 1968 he won acclaim for his part in a play centred on the Liverpool docks, 'The Big Flame'. One of his great loves had always been musicals. He appeared in 'Salad Days' and 'My Fair Lady'. In 1985 he started on a run of 567 consecutive appearances in 'Guys and Dolls'. He overtook this record in 1998 during a run of 'Beauty and the Beast' at the Dominion Theatre, London. It was during this time, in November 1998, that he was told that he had cancer. He died on 21 May 1999, leaving behind his second wife, Cindy, whom he had married just two months before.

*Leonard Rossiter, alias Mr Rigsby*

# Leonard Rossiter (1926-84)

A series of adverts for Cinzano, in which he poured water over Joan Collins, brought Leonard not only a good income, but also widespread acclaim. But even without this, he would still have been one of the country's best comedy actors, perhaps reaching his peak of performance in his portrayal of Mr Rigsby, the landlord, in 'Rising Damp'.

Any ambitions that Leonard had for going to university to study modern languages came adrift when his father John was killed during the war. Leonard had been born on 21 October 1926, the family living at 65 Montrovia Crescent in Fazakerley. He went to school at the Collegiate, but with his father's death, money needed to be earned to help support his mother Elizabeth. So for seven years he endured life as a clerk in the claims department of Commercial Union, based in a large white building opposite the town hall. His acting ability was apparent by his performances as an amateur with the East Wavertree Players, the Wavertree Community Centre Players and a group called Ad Astra in Speke.

In 1954 Leonard decided to turn professional. He started out with a two-year spell with Preston Repertory followed by periods at the Salisbury and Birmingham reps as well as Bristol Old Vic. His first London appearance was in 1958 in a small role in 'Free as the Air' at the Savoy Theatre. He came to Liverpool that year with the play at the

Royal Court and also 'The Ice Man Cometh' at the Shakespeare Theatre. At the start of the 60s he was in a number TV plays, including a
12-week period in 1961 as Inspector Bamber in 'Z Cars', set in Kirkby.
In the same year he was in the film 'A Kind of Loving'. Broadway
beckoned two years later, but the play, 'Semi-detached', lasted only
two weeks. He put it down to the different American sense of humour. 1964 saw an appearance in 'Steptoe & Son' and the play 'Justin
Thyme'.

Leonard gained the Variety Club award for best actor of 1969 for his
performance in 'The Resistable Rise Of Arturo Ui'. This brought him
to the attention of a wider public. After his divorce from his wife Josephine, he married Gillian Raine, an actress, in 1972. They had one
daughter Camilla. The family lived close to the Fulham Road, near
the Chelsea football ground. His TV popularity was based on his starring role in the 1976 BBC series 'The Rise and Fall of Reginald Perrin'.
Transferring to ITV, his prime achievement came in 1980 with 'Rising Damp'. At the same time he was taking part in a 12-month run of
the play 'Make And Break' at the Haymarket Theatre. His other TV series, 'The Loser', in which he played the part of a wrestling manager
did not attain the same heights. He returned to his old school, the Collegiate, for its prize-giving ceremony in 1981. Back at the Haymarket
Theatre in 1982, he appeared in Pirandello's 'The Rules Of The
Game'. By then hard work was beginning to take its toll on Leonard.
His last major role was in 1983 as King John in the BBC play. He died
of a heart attack on 5 October 1984 as he sat in the dressing room wait-
ing to go on stage in a performance of the play 'Loot'.

Always seeing himself as a comedy actor rather than a comedian,
Leonard was a shy man, who hated publicity. This to the extent that
he once refused to go on the Michael Parkinson TV chat show. He
worked hard as a member of the council of Equity, the actors' union.

# Patricia Routledge (1929- )

'If you are not seen on TV, then you must be dead,' seems to be the
opinion of the general public regarding those in the acting profession.
It is not realised that those who achieve apparent sudden TV fame
have often been working on stage for many years. This was certainly
the case as far as Patricia Routledge was concerned. She made her

name to a wider audience first of all as the posh Hyacinth Bucket (pronounced Bouquet) in the series 'Keeping Up Appearances'. (Her husband in the series was played by Clive Swift, another Merseysider. He and his actor brother David were both given honorary degrees at John Moores University in July 1999.) Then she successfully followed this as the homely Darwen detective in 'Hetty Wainthropp Investigates'.

Father Isaac ran a gents' outfitters at 36 Church Road in Higher Tranmere. Her mother was Catherine. The family lived at 2 Whitfield Street. Born on 17 February 1929, Pat went to Mersey Park council school. In a school play, she played the part of the hare in 'The Hare and the Tortoise'. Out of school, she joined a dancing class. Her parents often took her to see the stars of the day at the Argyle Theatre, Birkenhead. Although sadly on the receiving end of German bombs in the war, it was then the prime north-west theatre. The first pantomime she remembers seeing was Sandy Powell ('Can You Hear Me, Mother?') as Cinderella at the Empire Theatre. Attending Birkenhead Park High School, she took extra-curricular elocution and singing lessons. The English teacher, who took these, encouraged her love of the stage. She appeared in school plays, the first being 'The Critic' by Sheridan. Patricia went on to read English at Liverpool University, in the days when the number of women taking higher studies was comparatively low. Keeping up her interest in acting, she took the part of Lady Bracknell in the University Dramatic Society's production of Oscar Wilde's 'The Importance of Being Earnest'.

After graduating in English Literature and Language in 1951, Patricia's intention was to train as a teacher. This plan was changed after she had an successful audition at the Playhouse Theatre. Wondering whether she was doing the right thing or not, it was only a year later that she took up the offer. So uncertain had she been, that she had taken a course in shorthand typing as a stand by for the future. She progressed in her two years at the theatre from assistant stage manager to a full member of the company, making her first appearance in Shakespeare's *A Midsummer Night's Dream*.

Having learned her trade at the Playhouse, Patricia set off for the bright lights of London. Her debut was somewhat unexpected. One of the cast of Sheridan's play 'The Duenna', at the Westminster Theatre, was suddenly taken ill. Patricia jumped at the chance of replacing her. In the years immediately following, her experience widened to touring repertory, the Bristol Old Vic, musicals in the West End and a TV role as Mrs Snape in 'Coronation Street'. A part in Shakespeare's *Comedy of Errors* had been her debut on TV. Her role as the Queen in the 1964 four-part TV series 'Victoria Regina' was the one that brought her to the notice of a wider public. She played Victoria from a young girl to an 80-year-old. By 1968 she was playing in the musical 'Darling of the Day' on Broadway. Although she received great acclaim from the critics and won a Tony award, it had only a short run. This was followed by a musical about Queen Victoria in Los Angeles and an appearance in Gilbert and Sullivan's 'The Pirates of Penzance' in Central Park, New York.

*Patricia Routledge with an honorary degree presented at the Anglican Cathedral*

The scope of Patricia's activity extended to her first film part in the 1966 'To Sir, With Love' and then, with Dudley Moore, in 'Thirty Is a Dangerous Age'. In the same year, she returned to Broadway in the play 'How's The World Treating You?'. She again received critical acclaim for her role as three different wives. Her remarkable versatility is seen by the scope of her performances: in 1982 in Alan Bennett's monologue 'A Woman of No Importance', with the Royal Shakespeare Company in *Richard III* and in Berstein's 'Candide' with the Old Vic Company in 1988. In that year she received a BAFTA award for her part in Bennett's 'Lady of Letters'. Both of these monologues were then performed together as the 'Talking Heads' series. Her close association with Bennett was continued when she took part in the BBC production of 'Sophia and Constance'.

Patricia had been back in Liverpool to present the prizes at her old school in 1986. Two years later, she was again in Liverpool to try out her one-person show 'Come for the Ride' as part of the Festival of Comedy. She also tried it out at a fundraising event for a hospice in Worcester, before taking the show on a tour of Britain. Since then

'Keeping Up Appearances' and 'Hetty Wainthropp Investigates' have made her nationally famous.

One of the sadnesses of Patricia's life was very personal. After remaining unmarried for many years, she fell in love with someone she met in 1988. It was a blow when he died not long after. This was one of a number of bereavements. Her mother had died during the 1950s. Her father remarried, dying in 1984, four years after her stepmother. Then her brother, Graham, a canon of St Paul's Cathedral, died in 1990. In spite of these personal losses, Patricia has continued with her first love of acting, which has made her so popular. This popularity was recognised in 1993 when, in a ceremony at the Anglican Cathedral, she was granted an honorary degree by John Moores University. The same year she was awarded the OBE. In 1999, she was presented with an honorary degree by her old university.

Later in the year, Patricia revived her role as Lady Bracknell in 'The Importance of Being Earnest' at the Chichester Festival, followed by a successful run at the Haymarket, London.

# Lita Roza (1926- )

It was a cold evening in 1941. Fifteen-year-old Lita had been to the pictures. She was walking home along Lodge Lane, when a bomb fell. Injured in the leg by the flying shrapnel, she was taken to the Northern Hospital. The irony was that her parents had ordered her to return from a tour of the provinces she had been doing with Ted Ray, mistakenly thinking that she would be safer at home. Now Lita's budding career as a dancer was ended. If she was going to make it at all, it would have to be as a singer.

Born on 14 March 1926, one of seven children, her parents were both in show business. Her father Frank had worked at ICI Speke and then as a marine engineer. He became well known on the local club circuit as an accordionist and singer. Her mother Elizabeth had been a dancer. The family home was at 13 Upper Pitt Street, where they stayed until 1934. The next move was to Wordsworth Street. Lita went to St Michael's school in Frederick Street, then on to Granby Street School.

*Lita Roza listens attentively to her boss, band leader Ted Heath, along with fellow singers Dickie Valentine, Denis Lotis and Bobby Britton, backstage at the Liverpool Empire.*

Taken to the Pavilion Theatre, Lodge Lane at the age of six to see 'Jack and Jill', the thrill of the theatre made Lita vow to become a star. It was 35 years later that she returned to top the bill at the Pavilion. Her dream had come true. In 1937, after seeing an advert in the paper, she appeared in the panto 'Dick Whittington' at Norwich. This was followed, in successive years, by panto at the Theatre Royal, Chester and two at the Empire Theatre, Liverpool. Although all this meant time off school, she still managed to do well at her studies.

After leaving school, Lita had a number of jobs. First of all she worked at a florists in Lodge Lane, a pram shop in Renshaw Street and a shop called Petite, which was near to Lewis's. Finally, it was back to Lodge Lane, working at the Home & Colonial Store. She was so good at patting butter that she was sent to other stores to show the staff how to do it.

Lita's career took a step forward when she got a spot as a singer at The New Yorker restaurant in Lord Street, Southport. Then she decided to try her luck in London. After an audition with Harry Roy, the bandleader, she sang with his band at Coventry Hippodrome. The band was due to go abroad to play to the troops. Much to her disappointment, Lita was unable to go because her brother Harry had just been killed in action with the RAF.

An amazing event then took place. While the band was in Egypt, an RAF officer saw Lita's photograph and immediately fell in love with her. On returning to London, Flt. Lt. James Holland, who was American, sought Lita out. They married at Marylebone Registry Office on 27 July 1944. She was 18, he 28. Sadly, the fairy-story romance was not to last. James was posted to a remote village in Quebec, Canada as a flying instructor for British pilots. They moved on to Miami in Florida, where James was demobbed. He then started a business, which supplied planes to spread fertiliser or insecticide over fields. He worked so hard that Lita saw little of him. She tried to make her life less lonely and boring by singing with a band, but James refused to let this continue. They divorced and Lita returned to England in January 1950.

Through Ted Heath, another well-known bandleader of the time, Lita got work singing in the London clubs, although these were not the venues she would have chosen. She also sang with the band on the BBC. Records followed such as 'Allentown Jail', 'Blacksmith Blues' and a number one with 'How Much Is That Doggie In The Window?' in 1953.

Lita left the Heath band in 1954 to go solo. In the December, a tour of the USA culminated in an appearance on the Bob Hope Show. The following year she did a 40-week tour of Britain. She was now at the peak of her success. So busy was she that when she married Ronnie Hughes, who played trumpet in the Heath band, at Marylebone Registry Office, she had to go straight off afterwards for her spot at the Palladium. Unfortunately the marriage was not to last.

Until the late 50s, Lita was in great demand on radio, stage and TV. In December 1958 she appeared in 'Babes In The Wood' at the Pavilion Theatre, Liverpool. A tour of Australia in 1960 and cabaret in Las Vegas in 1961 brought her career at the top to an end. From then until the early 90s she concentrated on the club circuit. Lita was not the only member of the Roza family to have success. Her sister Alma sang at various times with the orchestras of Stanley Black, Geraldo and the Squadronaires. Lita now lives in retirement in the London area.

# Lily Savage (1958- )

Paul O'Grady is an outstanding drag artist in a tradition going back through Dannie Le Rue to Vesta Tilley and Hetty King. The O'Grady family lived at 28 Holly Grove in Tranmere. After attending St Anselm's College, Manor Hill, Paul had a variety of jobs, including working in a children's home in Kirkby and behind the bar in Manilla. His acting career started as an extra in Coronation Street. It was when he took his mother's maiden name Savage, and added Lily to it, that fame beckoned. Paul first appeared as Lily in 1985 at the Vauxhall pub in London. He based her on someone he had seen in a Sheffield market. A TV breakthrough came with appearances on Channel 4's 'The Big Breakfast' and 'Live From Lilydome' in 1995. The 'Lily Savage Show' on BBC TV was scripted by himself. It was this that made him a nationwide name. He hosted 'Blankety Blank' on TV from 1998. The same year, the Liverpool Empire was packed out for three nights for a return home. The following Christmas saw a lead role as Miss Hannigan, complete with American accent, in the revival of the musical 'Annie' at the Victoria Palace, London, which went on tour in 1999.

Paul lived for many years in the Vauxhall district of London. He bought a large house in Adlington, Kent in 1999 to add to a house in central London.

# Alexei Sayle (1952- )

As a writer, actor, broadcaster, TV presenter and comedian, Alexei has had a very varied career in the entertainment world. Born on 7 August 1952, he was the son of Joseph, a railway guard, and Malka, a pools clerk. His grandparents had emigrated from Russia. The family home was 5 Valley Road, Anfield. In 1957 Alexei went to Anfield Road Primary School, then on to Alsop Grammar School. This was followed by spells at Southport College of Art and Chelsea School of Art until 1974. Before getting a foothold in the media, he worked as a dishwasher, building worker, DHSS clerk, cleaner and part-time college lecturer. On 4 January 1974 he married Linda Rawsthorn at Brougham Terrace Registrar's Office. She came from Everton. Her father Noel a pipe fitter, hailed originally from Crosby.

*Alexei Sayle: a man of diverse talents*

The first TV success that Alexei had was in 1979 as the compere of the 'Comedy Store', which produced comedians such as Ben Elton and French and Saunders. 'The Young Ones' (1982 – 84), 'Alexei Sayle's Stuff' (1988-91) and the 'All New Alexei Sayle Show' (1988-94) led on to 'You Make Me Feel Like Dancing' and 'Alexei Sayle's Merry Go Round' in 1998. He took part in the 'Great Railway Journeys of the World' TV series in 1996. A TV film of 1995, 'Sorry About Last Night', was turned into a radio series in 1999. Alexei has written a number of books and contributed to a variety of magazines and newspapers, including *The Independent* and *Sunday Mirror*. He has also appeared in a number of films, amongst them 'Gorky Park' in 1963 and 'Indiana Jones and the Last Crusade' in 1989. In 1999 he appeared in the film 'Swing', along with Hugo Speer and Rita Tushingham.

# The Scaffold

In spite of the insistence of the three members that they were not a pop group, The Scaffold will undoubtedly be remembered for their two chart-topping records.

The Scaffold originated from the 1962 Merseyside Arts Festival, where Roger McGough and John Gorman met for the first time. A group of eight formed 'The Liverpool One Fat Lady All Electric Show', to present a mixed review of readings and sketches. Then, after calling itself 'Bingo 8' and 'Liverpool 8', 'The Scaffold' emerged. One evening in December 1963, the group was performing at the Blue Angel Club. A TV agent chose three, Roger, John and Mike McGear, to take part in an ITV Saturday satirical show called 'Gazette'. At the Edinburgh Festival of 1964, the group put on a show called 'Birds, Marriages and Deaths'.

They turned professional in 1964 and Brian Epstein signed up the group in 1965. After a year, by mutual consent, Noel Gay in London took over management. Mike McGear, the brother of Paul McCartney, was born in Walton Hospital on 7 January 1944. After attending the Liverpool Institute, he took jobs as a Catholic Bible representative, a tailor and hairdresser. He was the composer of the hit 'Thank U Very Much'. Living on the Wirral, he has since become a photographer and author.

Roger McGough, born on 1 November 1937 in Litherland, was educated at St Mary's College, Crosby and Hull University. After teaching, he became a poet and playwright. His first full-length play, 'The Commission', was performed at the Everyman Theatre in 1967. In 1968 he wrote his first book 'Summer with Monica'. After the Scaffold heyday, he concentrated on poetry. He wrote, with Adrian Henri and Brian Patten 'The Mersey Sound', a best seller. In 1997 he was awarded the OBE. 1999 saw a new play 'The Sound Collector', a book 'The Way Things Are' plus an honorary degree at John Moores University. He has lived in Barnes since 1982, with his second wife and four children.

John Gorman, born in Birkenhead on 4 January 1937, went to St Anselm's College, followed by National Service. After being a post office engineer, he owned a boutique in Hackins Hey off Dale Street.

In 1965 the group did a two-week stint at the Establishment Club in London, as well as playing the Traverse Theatre at the Edinburgh Festival. They also appeared one evening per week at the Sink Club in Leece Street. In April that year some of their sketches went out on an American ITV programme called 'Hullabaloo'. In November they did a 16-venue tour with the 'Marquee Show'. Then 'Thank U Very Much' got into the top ten in 1967. The mysterious reference in the song to the 'Aintree Iron' was one that the group members always refused to explain. When, the following year, the group took an old American folk song and put new words to it, 'Lily the Pink' became a number one hit.

The group showed a concern for local talent by setting up an agency, Pink Music Ltd in 1969. A little later, they opened their own arts centre in Renshaw Street. In the summer of 1970, they undertook a series with the BBC, 'Score with the Scaffold'. A venture into films in 1971 saw the release of a short production, 'Plod', featuring, as the name implies, the police. Along with local poets such as Adrian

Henri, the group composed a show called 'Grimms', which began a 16-town tour at Liverpool University in March 1972. After this the group members began to follow their own individual pursuits, although not before another entry into the charts in 1974 with 'Liverpool Lou'.

# The Spinners

'In My Liverpool Home' they sang, but only one member of the group originated from Liverpool. Nonetheless, they all finished up living on Merseyside. The Spinners were soon adopted as Scousers, seen by their loyal following as sons of Liverpool.

The one genuine Liverpudlian was Hughie Jones. Born in 1936 in the south end of the city, his father was Welsh. The singing tradition of that country, plus the fact that his mother was a music teacher, made it almost inevitable that he would be a musician. After a time in Canada, he returned to Liverpool. He used to go along to the Spinners club with his guitar. One night he was asked to join in. The rest of the group were so impressed that, when Stan Francis left, Hughie was asked to join on a permanent basis. A trainee in factory management by day, he spent much time researching old folk songs and sea shanties. In 1963 he married Christine, making their home in Padstow Road, Childwall.

Many thought that Tony Davis was the leader of the group. Maybe his 6ft 8in presence made it look that way, but the Spinners worked on a democratic basis. He hailed from Blackburn. The family moved to 34 Thirlmere Drive, Wallasey when Tony was three. A jazz enthusiast from school days at Wallasey Grammar School, he learned to play the clarinet. After National Service, he had a number of jobs. One of these was at the Atomic Energy establishment in Capenhurst, where he first met up with Cliff Hall. He eventually trained as a teacher, taking up a post at Major Street School. He had run a number of jazz bands before joining up with Beryl, his wife, and Mick Groves to form the Gin Mill Skiffle Group, which played at the Cavern along with the Quarrymen and others.

Mick Groves came from Salford. He had met up with Tony Davis at teacher training college, where they became close friends. In Liverpool he took up successive teaching posts at Westminster Road RC,

All Souls, off Scotland Road, St Gregory's and St Francis Xaviour schools. In the summer of 1962, he and Tony went to the USA to do some concerts at the invitation of Pete Seeger. Cliff had to be left behind because he could not get time off work. When they got back, Mick married Margaret Parry, who worked on the door at the Spinners club, at St Francis Xaviour church. He was the first Spinner to broadcast when he appeared on BBC's 'Guitar Club'.

Cliff Hall was from further afield. An electrician by trade, he was born in 1936 in Oriente, Cuba, although his family was Jamaican. After they returned to Jamaica, he came to Britain in 1942 to serve for three years in the RAF. Deciding to stay in this country, he married Janet Massie, a Glaswegian, in 1947. Five years later they moved to Liverpool to live at 15 Violet Street. Tony Davis, after their meeting at Capenhurst, recruited him. His knowledge of West Indian songs, plus his ability on guitar and harmonica, made him a valuable asset to the group.

Beryl Davis and Stan Francis were early members of the group, as was Jacqui McDonald, who studied at LM Marsh college. Leaving the group in 1961, she was later part of the well-known Jacqui and Bridie duo. Gin Mill became the Spinners when they were invited to per-

*A Shrove Tuesday in Ormskirk with The Spinners. Left to right: Mick Groves, Cliff Hall, Tony Davis and Hughie Jones*

form in May 1958 at the Conservative fête held at the cricket ground in Aigburth. They attracted so much attention that the stallholders asked them to stop, because they were losing business. From this point, the group started to concentrate on performing British and European folk songs rather than American. Soon after the Spinners Club was formed. It started off by hiring a room at Sampson and Barlow's' restaurant in London Road. Because of growing numbers, a move was made to Gregson's Well in Brunswick Road in 1963 and then to the Triton in 1975. The club was important to the development of the Spinners, since it was a place that they could try out new material. By now the group were also keen members of the English Folk and Dance Society, which met at the Friends' Meeting House in Paradise Street.

The group travelled from venue to venue by a van, driven by Cliff on routes planned by Mick. Tony was made responsible for the booking of engagements, with Hughie looking after the money side. Club membership rose to 2000, the Spinners magazine being sent to subscribers all over the world. Each year a birthday concert was held at the St George's Hall. The first broadcast was on the 'Roundabout' programme, the same year that they were involved in helping the local drive to encourage X-rays, by singing 'TB or not TB'.

1961 was a busy year. The group appeared at the Fritz Speigal Festival of Liverpool songs at the Bluecoat Chambers. Then they did their first BBC series, followed by a visit the USA. Early in 1962, Tony Davis was asked to sing on television a song he had written when he noticed how tired some of his pupils were. It was called 'Lure of TV'. That year the group took part in the TV series 'Dance 'n Skylark'. In April 1964 the first LP, simply called 'The Spinners', was released. Three months later, two LPs from a concert recorded at the Philharmonic Hall, 'Folk at the Phil' and 'More Folk at the Phil' were produced. In the September the group took the risky decision to turn professional. Travelling was not without its pitfalls. In December 1965, because of fog, the group arrived late at Centre '63 in Kirkby from a distant booking, only to find the audience had gone home. They returned the following evening to do the show.

The group set off for a tour in Denmark for two weeks in March 1967. In October they appeared in the TV Sunday programme 'Grief and Glory'. The Playhouse was empty at the beginning of 1968 because the current show had been taken to St Helens for a week. The Spinners filled the gap with performances each night. 1968 saw the first of two TV series from the Octagon Theatre in Bolton and a series on radio 'The Spinners and Friends'. When the Queen came to open the Kingsway Tunnel in 1971, the Spinners sang at the celebratory concert at the Empire Theatre.

Bill Brown was the bass player. As the workload increased, he began to share the task with 'Count' John McCormick. When Brown left the group in 1974, John became full-time, also acting as music arranger. Although he has never liked the title, he became known as the fifth Spinner.

The group split up by mutual agreement in 1989, deciding to concentrate on their own individual interests. It reckoned to have a repertoire of 2000 songs. The £5,000 profit from their farewell concert held on Christmas Eve 1988 at the Phil went to the work of Mother Teresa, a cause that had been dear to their hearts for over 20 years. Although Cliff now lived in Kent after the death of his wife Janet, the group re-united for end of the year tours for the next three years.

# Freddie Starr (1943- )

'Freddie Starr ate my hamster,' were the newspaper accusations of an apparently incensed lady in March 1986. The fact that he was supposed to have eaten it in a sandwich did not lessen her wrath. True or not, it was the sort of thing that many believed this manic comedian from Old Swan would get up to. Born Fred Fowell at 61 Wharncliffe Road on 9 January 1943, he went to secondary school in Huyton. Multi-talented, he made his name first of all as a singer and impressionist. At school, he was remembered more for his impersonating the teachers than learning anything from them. From the age of eight, he was always willing to put on a comedy or song and dance show. After working on building sites and trying his hand at boxing, he embarked on a show business career. At the age of 14, he appeared in a Rank Liverpool based film 'The Violent Playground', but this was a one-off.

While getting an income as a furniture salesman, he sang with a backing group The Midnighters, which was the stage at which he changed his name to Freddie Starr. In 1963 he formed another group The Thunderbirds, appearing with them at the Stanley Stadium in September of that year. They then followed the route of the Beatles and others, by appearing at the Star Club in Hamburg. Brian Epstein was obviously not impressed, because he refused to sign them up.

Changing backing groups almost as often as he changed his socks, Freddie went with the Delmonts to entertain the forces in Aden and Cyprus and then in May 1967 went on a Canadian tour, including a booking at Expo '67 in Montreal. Freddie had first heard the group on a rainy night. He had gone into the Mardi Gras club, where they were performing. He got up on stage to do some impressions, thus beginning an association with the group that lasted for five years. Af-

*Freddie Starr: the manic comedian*

ter an appearance on 'Opportunity Knocks' and a summer season in Rhyl, Freddie decided to go solo. His first booking was at the Kingsway, Southport.

The little bit of luck needed to get noticed came when he stood in for Dick Emery one night in Manchester. An impresario, who happened to be in the audience, immediately booked him for a six-week spell at the London Palladium. From then on the work flowed in – a show with Dora Bryan in Glasgow, a season at the Opera House Blackpool with the Bachelors and a Royal Command Performance in 1969. Two years previously a son Kari was born to Freddie and his wife Betty. By 1970 the family had moved to their home in Woodchurch Road, Birkenhead. The marriage broke up and Freddie then married Sandy Morgan, a dancer he had met at a Great Yarmouth summer show in 1974. They went to live in Windsor.

Freddie started to make his TV name by appearing on 'Who Do You Do?' for four years from 1972, with his impressions of anyone from Adolf Hitler to Elvis Presley. He topped the bill at the Palladium again in 1976. Then things began to go drastically wrong. In the early 80s, he revealed that he had been a drug addict for a number of years. He said that he had been well under the influence when an ITV programme, 'Freddie Starr on the Road' was filmed in 1981. He had got to such a state that he had to be replaced on his 'Madhouse' TV comedy series by Russ Abbot. At one stage he had debts of almost £200,000. To make matters worse, in 1984 he accused John Stewart, his manager who came from Dovecot, of assaulting him at the Holiday Inn in Birmingham. A court case ensued. To cap it all, he lost a lot of money in a multi-million-property speculation in Spain. He announced he was retiring from show business.

On the basis that it is impossible to keep a good man down, Freddie gradually started to work again. Although in the '90s he never regained his previous TV pre-eminence, he made an increasing number of guest appearances on other people's programmes. In 1999 he appeared in Sky TV's 'Beat the Crusher'. In August 1999 Freddie had a serious car accident on the M4 in Berkshire, but recovered to continue his summer season in Devon.

# Ringo Starr (1940- )

The vast horde of Irish immigrants into Liverpool in the 19th century is better remembered than that of the Welsh, yet many of the Victorian Liverpool streets were built by builders from that land. Wedged between South Street and High Park Street in Toxteth are what are known locally as 'the Welsh Streets'. One of these is Madryn Street. The author remembers it well because he began married life at number 40. Number 9 was more famous, because it was here that Ringo was born as Richard (Richie) Starkey on 7 July 1940. He bore the same name as his father, who had married Elsie Gleave in 1936 at the long demolished St Silas's Church, which stood next to the still-thriving school.

The marriage lasted only seven years. After the divorce, Elsie and Ringo moved the short distance to 10 Admiral Grove, just off the other side of High Park Street. To earn much-needed extra cash, Elsie worked in the nearby Empress pub. Years later, it was to feature on the cover of the album 'Sentimental Journey'. Ringo went to St Silas's School on the corner of High Park Road and Admiral Street. One of his best friends there was Ronny Wycherley (Billy Fury). In their final year, a first-year pupil was Valerie Jones, later the author's wife. Ringo's schooling was much interrupted by illness. In 1946 he found himself in the Children's Hospital in Myrtle Street for a number of months.

At 11 Ringo went on to Dingle Vale Secondary School (now Shorefields), where the author taught part-time in the mid-sixties. His previous illness had put him so far behind in his education that he felt increasingly out on a limb. This feeling encouraged him to play truant, being more often found in the cinema than the classroom. A severe attack of pleurisy in his mid-teens put him back in the Children's Hospital, followed by a long convalescence in the Children's Hospital in Heswall. Meanwhile, his mother Elsie had got married in 1953 to Harry Greaves. Coming up from Romford, he was by trade a painter working for Liverpool Corporation. Ringo saw little of his natural father, who kept his distance during the whole of his son's career.

After leaving school at 15, Ringo went from job to job, including one on railway deliveries, another as barman on the New Brighton Ferry and finally as an apprentice joiner at the engineering firm of Henry Hunt. It did not look as if he could stick at anything. Music came to his rescue. A childhood enthusiasm for using cardboard boxes as drums had led his stepfather to buy him a drum. Ringo joined Rory Storm and the Hurricanes in November 1959. In their previous incarnation they had been Alan Caldwell's Texan Skiffle group. Ringo had been playing with groups for a couple of years by then, having made his first public appearance with the Eddie Clayton Skiffle Group at the Peel Street Labour Club. He then performed with some regularity at the Florence Institute, no more than half a mile away from home.

Decision time came in 1960. The group was offered a season at Butlin's holiday camp in Pwllheli. He decided to hand in his notice at Hunt's, hoping that the Butlin's season would lead on to something else. It did. During that first season, the members of the group were given more exotic-sounding names to add to the hype. Starr seemed a good stage name and, because of the rings he wore, Ringo was added to it. After a second Butlin's season, the group followed the Liverpool exodus to Hamburg, along with the Beatles. Back home there was no lack of bookings. By 1962 they were not only appearing locally from Southport to New Brighton, but also in bracing Skegness and sunny Marbella.

By now Ringo was a very marketable commodity. He had had a

short spell with Tony Sheridan and the Star Combo in Hamburg. Back home, Kingsize Taylor wanted Ringo to join his group, but the offer he succumbed to was to replace Pete Best, just sacked by the Beatles. He made his debut for them at a horticultural society function in Birkenhead on 18 August 1962.

During his Beatles career, Ringo was seen by Lennon and McCartney as the man who sat at the back of the stage, contributing little else than his drumming. It is no coincidence that he was closer to George Harrison than the other two. On his own, after the break up of the group, he never matched even the sometimes-limited achievements of the other three. Although he appeared, with a star-studded cast, in the film 'The Magic Christian' and issued 'Yellow Submarine' as a single, the impact was small.

By now a wealthy man, Ringo, Maureen and their three children, Zac, John and Jason lived in a large house in Compton Avenue, Highgate. Maureen Cox had been his childhood sweetheart. When they first met, she was living at 56d Boundary Road and working at the Ashley du Pré saloon as a hairdresser. Ringo continued his efforts in the recording studios with a single 'It Don't Come Easy' and LPs 'Ringo Starrdust' and 'Beaucoups of Blues'. None set the world on fire. After making an appearance at the charity concert for Bangladesh, organised by George Harrison at Madison Square Garden, New York on 1 August 1971, Ringo turned his attention to films. He played the part of a bandit in the western 'Blindman'. He then directed 'Born to Boogie' in 1972. Production of a horror movie 'Son of Dracula' turned out to be a costly mistake. It seemed that his destiny was not to be in the acting in, direction of or production of films.

From this point, his life started on a downward slope. In September 1973 he had purchased the vast Tittenhurst Park in Ascot from John Lennon. But he chose to spend most of his time in the USA, leaving Maureen in England. After he had indulged in an affair with Nancy Andrews, the inevitable divorce took place on 17 July 1975. Ringo then had the bright idea of setting up a record company, which he did in April 1976. It lasted just over two years. Ill health returned to haunt him. On 13 April 1979 he was admitted to hospital in Monte Carlo with a repeat of his childhood peritonitis.

In 1981 Ringo tried his hand at films again. Although his appearance in a comedy 'Caveman' was inauspicious, he fell in love with one of the actresses, Barbara Bach. They were drawn closer together by the fact that, driving on the Kingston bypass, they were involved in an accident that could have been fatal. Marriage took place at Marylebone Registry Office on 27 April 1981.

Revd Wilber Awdry's books about 'Thomas the Tank Engine' had been transferred to the TV screen, with Johnny Morris as narrator. When he retired, Ringo surprisingly took his place. Even more surprisingly, he was a success. With suitable transatlantic alterations, the series went on the USA network. This time Ringo was the voice of 'Mr. Conductor'. By now both Ringo and Barbara were drinking very heavily. They decided in October 1988 to enter a clinic for alcoholics. They came out as zealous teetotallers. So great was the reform that Barbara opened a clinic in London in 1991.

# Richard Stilgoe (1943- )

Not a Liverpudlian by birth, Richard and his family lived in Surrey before moving to Liverpool. At school at Quarry Bank, he was leader of the group Tony Snow and the Blizzard, one of the many on the scene at the time. However, it was good enough to appear higher on the bill at the Cavern than the Beatles in 1960. After school, he won a naval scholarship to Dartmouth. He gave up after two weeks, going to Cambridge University instead. There he started studying engineering before changing to reading a music degree. The direction of his future career was set by his stage experience with the university Footlights Club.

In the mid-60s, Richard got together with Glyn Worsnip to do review work, which he both wrote and appeared in. They went down so well with the customers of the London Restaurant that their booking was extended. This approach was transferred to the TV in 'A Class of His Own' followed by the series 'A Kick up the Eighties'. He made regular appearances on 'That's Life' and 'Nationwide'. In the latter, he renewed acquaintance with Glyn Worsnip and also Bernard Falk, who had been a guitarist in his Liverpool group.

Richard first appeared on radio in 1964, making his mark over the years with 'The Year In Question' and 'Stilgoe's Around'. More recently he has written the words for 'Starlight Express' by Andrew Lloyd Webber.

# Jimmy Tarbuck (1940- )

*Jimmy Tarbuck: entertainer & golfer*

'Tarby' now spends more time on the golf course than he does on the stage. Eric Sykes once commented, 'Jimmy is known for two things – his golf and his act. I don't know which is the funnier.' It was during a summer season in Blackpool that Jimmy caught his enthusiasm for golf from Bruce Forsyth. A Liverpool comedian, contemporary with the Beatles, he made it to the top at a time that Liverpool mania was all the rage. A Scouse accent was now an advantage rather than a drawback.

There was a show business lineage in the family. Jimmy's mother, Frances, had been on the stage for a number of years. She had first appeared in the panto 'Jack and the Beanstalk' at the Rotunda Theatre in Stanley Road. Father Fred was a bookmaker. So the combination of stage and money was a good pointer to Jimmy's future career. Born on 6 February 1940, he went to Dovedale Road School, where George Harrison was a fellow pupil. He had a sister Norma and brother, Ken. Sadly another brother Freddie died when young. Senior school was St Frances Xaviour's, from which he was expelled for missing lessons. So he transferred to Rose Lane Secondary, where he stayed until he was 15. A variety of jobs followed, as he tried his hand at most things. These included milk boy, butcher's boy, hairdressing, working in a laundry, and a short-lived spell as a garage mechanic. It was pretty obvious that the young Jimmy was not cut out for the humdrum 9 to 5 existence of the majority.

The opportunity to go on the stage arose by accident. In 1958 Jimmy was staying at Butlin's in Pwllheli with a few footballing friends from Liverpool FC. At a talent competition, he did not think much of the acts, giving them a dose of verbal stick. He was challenged, if he thought he could do any better, to have a go himself, so he jumped up on the stage, making up his act as he went along. Much to his surprise, he won. This meant returning for the next round, which he did, winning again. From there he won through the regional finals in Blackpool and went to the national finals, held at the Park Lane Hotel in London. He did not win, but he had accumulated more money en route than he had ever earned before, getting some free holidays into the bargain. As far as he was concerned, there was no turning back.

By 1959 the world seemed to be at Jimmy's feet. He married Pauline Carfoot in the September and then went on tour for 12 weeks with a show starring the country's leading singers and groups. But then the bookings dried up, except for a few one-night stands at Manchester clubs. Things were so bad that he went back to Butlin's at Pwllheli, where he worked in the kitchens, as well as taking part in the shows that were put on by the Redcoats. Pauline was also there, working in the shop at the camp. Luckily, he was seen by someone who offered him a job as resident comic at the Ocean Hotel in Saltdean, Sussex. His continuing enthusiasm for football also got him into the reserve team at Brighton and Hove Albion. The high spot was scoring five times in one of the matches.

More hard times followed. Jimmy was sacked from a job he found in London because his Liverpool accent was disliked. He managed to get a few club bookings back on Merseyside. His father gave Jimmy some money to enable him to get a car, so that he could get from venue to venue. A talent contest was being held at the Floral Pavilion, New Brighton, so Jimmy entered, using the name Andy King. This led to a week at the Pavilion Theatre, Lodge Lane. By now he had been taken on by an agent, George Ganjou. He got Jimmy a week's work at the Metropole Music Hall on the Edgware Road in London, where Max Miller was topping the bill. Jimmy learned a lot from the week, particularly not to let himself lose his temper with hecklers. On tour soon after, at Burnley, he was hit by an ice cream thrown from the audience. A riot ensued which necessitated police intervention. For Jimmy, it was a sharp learning curve.

The road to TV fame was opened up by the opportunity of recording a trial tape at the ATV studios in Manchester. Meanwhile, Jimmy was booked for a summer season at Arbroath. The show came to a grinding halt when audiences failed to materialise. Life for Jimmy seemed to be pretty grim again. But almost as soon as the Arbroath show closed, his new agent, Merseysider Terry Miller, let him know that the TV bosses had been impressed by his audition. Soon he made his TV debut in 'Comedy Bandbox' in October 1963.

Although working hard to make a decent living, Jimmy gave many shows for charity. In December 1964 the Broadway Club in Norris Green was the venue for a presentation by the Liverpool Working Men's Clubs. Jimmy received a gold watch for his services to charity. He was in Liverpool again for the Christmas pantomime 'Puss in Boots' at the Empire Theatre.

The Palladium is the mecca of all artists. To play there is to have reached the peak of achievement. Jimmy made his first appearance on 28 October 1963. He overran his time slot, with the result that Xavier Cugat and his band, the stars of the evening, had to reduce theirs. This was only a foretaste of greater things to come. After a successful summer season in Great Yarmouth, he was chosen to replace Bruce Forsyth as compere for the TV series 'Sunday Night at the Palladium'. This he did for 39 weeks. One of his most difficult evenings occurred when Judy Garland refused to go on stage. As the pit orchestra played 'Over the Rainbow' again and again, Jimmy had to cajole her into action.

By now, Jimmy was at the peak of his profession. With Pauline and their children Cheryl, Lisa (now a TV star herself) and Jimmy junior, he had a large house in Surrey and a villa in Marbella. Besides his media work, he owned a garage in Liverpool and was director of an electrical goods firm besides having considerable property assets. In addition, he and Frankie Vaughan jointly owned some racehorses. He also bought a house on the Wirral for his parents.

Now there was no worry about getting work. On the contrary, Jimmy had to take a break from his hectic schedule. In 1964 he had the honour of being chosen for the Royal Variety Show. Four years later he was back at the Palladium in the pantomime 'Jack and the Beanstalk' with fellow Liverpudlian Arthur Askey. The accolade of the red book came with 'This is Your Life' in 1983. He continued to be in great demand for TV, with 'Live from Her Majesty's' (1983-5), 'Tarby and Friends' (1984-6) and 'Live from the London Palladium' (1987-8). 'Winner Takes All' was a favourite amongst a number of TV quiz games he hosted. These days Jimmy is seen on the golf course more than the stage.

# Ian Tracey (1955- )

*Ian Tracey: master of the organ console*

To be able to attract 2000 people to Liverpool Anglican Cathedral for an organ recital at 11am on an Easter Monday morning year by year is no mean feat, but such is the musical skill of Ian that he can do just that. At the age of 25 he became the youngest cathedral organist in the country, when he was appointed to succeed Noel Rawsthorne at Liverpool. Born at Elmswood Nursing Home on 27 May 1955, his Scottish father William was a watchmaker and jeweller, and mother Helene a social worker from Merseyside. The family lived at 12 Liddell Road, West Derby. They then moved to 38 Corinthian Avenue, where Ian attended the nearby primary school from 1960 to 1966. Subsequently, he lived at 67 Beauclair Drive and 55 Rodney Street. Further education was Highfield School, which he left in 1973 for two years of study at Trinity College, London. He then studied for a while in France, before a year at St Katherine's College in Woolton.

A professional musician from the start of his working career, Ian was director of music at St Edmund's College from 1976 to 1982 and lecturer in music at C.F. Mott College for the following six years. From 1980 he had also undertaken the task of cathedral organist, with the role of Master of Choristers added two years later. He gradually began to build an impressive reputation as a recitalist both in Europe and the USA. It is the Queen's privilege to nominate a cathedral organist to play each year at the Service of Remembrance at the Royal Albert Hall. In 1983 Ian was the first organist to represent Liverpool at the event. He has appeared on a number of occasions at the Promenade Concerts at the Royal Albert Hall, frequently broadcast for the BBC, and made many records for EMI. In addition to all this, he manages to be consultant organist at St George's Hall, chorus master of the Royal Liverpool Philharmonic Society and Professor, Fellow and Organist at Liverpool John Moores University.

# Rita Tushingham (1942- )

'The Ugly Duckling' was the name the press gave to Rita. She was never likely to vie with Hollywood stars in the good looks stakes, but she proved that talent is more important than being a front-runner in the beauty parade. She was born on 14 March 1942, the daughter of John and Enid. The family home was 2 Ashton Drive, Hunts Cross. Her father ran a grocer's shop and post office at 176 Garston Old Road. Rita used to help out in the shop on Saturday mornings. Father was also keen on football. Along with her brothers, Colin and Peter, Rita had the unusual experience of being taken both to Anfield and Goodison Park. The family was very much involved in the community. Her father was elected to the city council at a 1960 by-election, following in his father's footsteps. He also President of the Garston Rotary Club and Woolton Boys' Club. A member of the St Columba's Presbyterian Church Dramatic Society, Rita first appeared on stage at the age of four as a dancer. At school at La Sagesse Convent in Aigburth, she appeared in a number of plays. Further stage training took place at the Shelagh Elliot-Clarke School.

Rita then went to The Playhouse as assistant stage-manager. This post was supposed to be a temporary one, but lasted for two years. It was a 12 hours a day job, but excellent basic stage training. A major part of the job was setting up and then clearing away the stage furniture. Her appearances on the stage in between were somewhat restricted, amounting to no more than the back legs of a horse in 'Aladdin', the role of a rabbit in 'Toad of Toad Hall' and minor parts in Shaw's 'Pygmalion' and Ben Traver's 'Thark'. There was a more substantial role in a play 'I Remember, I Remember', which was based on 19th-century Ormskirk. A prophecy about the future came when Sybil Thorndike saw her at a Playhouse event. Part of it was a sketch entitled 'William Square Dance', in which Rita imitated Ruby Murray. The Thorndike verdict was that Rita was someone worth keeping an eye on for the future. Not sure of how secure her future career would be, Rita's parents persuaded her to take a shorthand-typing course as a standby.

It was 1961. Film director, Tony Richardson, was looking for someone to play the part of Jo in 'A Taste of Honey'. The story, about an unmarried mother and a seaman, took place in Salford. Dora Bryan played the part of Jo's mother. Rita was one of 2000 hopefuls who answered an advert for the role. Richardson was searching for an actress who had plain looks. Rita, small in stature with a turned-up nose, fitted the bill. Her drama tutor, Harold Ackerly, had rehearsed her for the audition, with various set pieces. Rita was one of the final ten, but was turned down. The director, having second thoughts, asked her back. The job was hers. The film was acclaimed by both critics and public. The premiere was at the Odeon Leicester Square, London on 14 September 1961, followed by Liverpool on 29 October. Rita had been on tour with the play 'The Knack', later to be made into a film. She joined in the pre-film supper at the Royal Court. All this should have led to Rita being in great demand. The opposite was the case. For almost two years she had very little work, except for a part in *A Midsummer Night's Dream* in London. Then her luck began to turn again.

Three films came Rita's way in quick succession. 'The Leather Boys' was about a girl who loved motorcycling. 'A Place To Go' and 'The Lonely Girl' followed. In March 1962 she was voted Variety Club newcomer of the year. During filming in Ireland in May 1963, she felt ill. This was diagnosed as stress due to overwork. She was forced to rest. Soon after the making of 'The Leather Boys', she secretly married Terry Bicknell on 1 December 1962. He had had a varied career, having been a salesman, clerk and stage electrician before becoming a TV cameraman. This job he gave up after the wedding to become Rita's manager. A family reception to celebrate the wedding was held at the Heath Hall Conservative Hall in Allerton.

Although the films Rita had done after 'A Taste of Honey' had been adequate, they had not packed the customers into the cinema seats. However, her next two won great acclaim where it counts – at the Cannes Film Festival. In 1964, she won the best actress award for 'Girl With Green Eyes', which also starred Peter Finch. A family celebration took place on 14 July, when Rita attended her brother Colin's marriage to Rita Farnworth, from 68 Holt Hill in Birkenhead, at St Stephen's Church in Prenton. The following year, 'The Knack', a comedy along with Michael Crawford, won the award for the best film of the year. This was the year she also starred in the MGM hit movie 'Dr Zhivago', followed in 1966 by 'The Trap'.

After marriage, Rita and Terry first of all made home in Earl's Court. A daughter, Dodonno, was born on 1 May 1964. On the birth of their second daughter, Aisha, in 1971, the family moved to a 16th-century cottage in Essex. Finally, it was on to a house, with a minstrel's gallery overlooking the sea, on the cliffs near Polperro in Cornwall. Filming continued in 1967 with the release of 'Smashing Time', co-starring Lynn Redgrave, and 'The Guru'. The latter was made in India with Michael Redgrave. In 1974 she appeared on TV in 'No Strings' by Carla Lane, the Liverpool writer. The two women struck up a long-lasting friendship. Although her film career continued to prosper, Rita's marriage ran into problems. Divorce led to her marrying Ossie Rawi, who ran a TV company, at Regent's Park mosque on 27 August 1981. She converted to become a Moslem. The couple went to live in Canada in 1980.

Roles were by now more difficult to come by. A number of films that Rita made were never seen in Britain. With Ossie as director, she made a Ruth Rendell mystery, 'A Judgement In Stone'. They came to Britain in 1987 to publicise it. At the same time Rita had a part in the play 'Children, Children' in Cardiff. The following year, she appeared in an ITV series about the Falklands War. Then Carla Lane asked her to make an appearance in her popular TV series 'Bread'. Rita played the part of a refined Liverpudlian. In 1999, she appeared in the Liverpool film 'Swing'.

# Frankie Vaughan (1928-99)

'Give Me The Moonlight' will be forever associated with Liverpool's Mr. Entertainment, Frankie Vaughan. Picked up in a Glasgow music shop in 1918, the song epitomised his silky top hat and cane performances. Born Frankie Ableson on 3 February 1928, the family lived at 35 Devon Street, off London Road. When he eventually chose the stage name Vaughan, he said it was because his grandmother called him her 'number vorn grandson'. When Frankie was eight years old his father Isaac took an upholsterer's shop on the corner of Lodge Lane, with the family moving to 45 Eversley Street, off Granby Street. His father was the son of a Russian immigrant from Kiev, who had in later life been a wrestler, worked in the diamond mines in South Africa and been an interpreter for the British in the Boer war. He was fluent in five languages. Because of his work for the British, he was allowed to come to England and settled in the Edge Lane area.

Frankie attended Prescot Street School and the Harrison-Jones school. In between times, for a while he belonged to a young gang who specialised in stealing goods from market stalls. After 18 months in Eversley Street, the family moved to Smithdown Road, where it was later bombed out. While he lived there, Frankie was a member of the choir of the synagogue in Princes Road, where he earned 12s 6d a week.

Since his father and mother, a seamstress, both worked, it was Frankie's grandmother, Mrs Kozak, who looked after him during the day. She took him all over the Merseyside – the Pier Head, New Brighton, Woolton Park and the museum and art gallery. Soon he was going with his school pals all over Liverpool – playing on the Cast Iron shore in the Dingle; to the shows at the Pavilion Theatre, Lodge Lane; to the pictures at the King's Cinema; to the swimming baths in Tunnel Road and the traditional walk round Aintree racecourse the day before the Grand National. Saturday afternoons were either spent at Paddy's Market or at the match at Anfield.

The next move was away from Liverpool, first of all evacuated with the family to Endmoor in Cumberland, then to Lancaster. Here Frankie attended the Boys' National School and joined the Lancaster Boys' Club. This was to be the start of a life-long association with boys clubs. At the Lancaster club he learned to box, was captain of the football team and played table tennis for Lancashire. It was here that he also sang in public for the first time, 'Old Father Thames' being the chosen song. Leaving school at 14, he won a scholarship to the Lancaster College of Art two years earlier than the normal age. The thesis he used to pass the entrance exam was on the subject of the Liver Buildings. The scholarship was transferred to the Leeds College, when the family moved to live at 78 Lewis Street.

Frankie's call up to the forces was deferred until he reached the intermediate stage of his course. He then joined the Royal Army Medical Corps for 3 years, stationed in Egypt and Malta. Since he served on a corvette, he reckoned he was both in the Army and the Navy. Back in Leeds, Frankie met his wife-to-be on his first night back home. His sister Myra had asked him to accompany her and a friend to the Locarno Ballroom in Leeds. Frankie preferred to go out with his mates to the local cinema. When they got there they found it was full, so he made his way to the Locarno to join Myra and her friend. The friend's name was Stella, and she was studying chemistry at the university. Three months later, on 6 June 1951, she and Frankie were married, honeymooning in Paignton. His father also served in the forces, but had been invalided out, returning to his timber firm in Leeds.

*Frankie Vaughan and his wife Stella*

On making his stage debut at the Empire, Leeds, during the university rag week, Frankie was spotted by the BBC producer Barney Colehan who advised him to turn professional. But in spite of winning a song contest at the Locarno and doing a BBC audition, he was unable to make a breakthrough.

Realising that his Art Teacher's Diploma would never earn him much money, Frankie turned his attention to commercial art as a potentially more lucrative occupation. After trailing around the shops in London, he managed to get an order to design a stand at the Earl's Court Exhibition, but nothing followed. It was not long before Frankie and Stella were broke. Something else had to be found quickly. Then Frankie remembered a letter of introduction to the impresario Bernard Delfont. The son of the manager of the City of Leeds Variety Theatre had given this to him, after his Leeds rag-week appearance at the Empire Theatre.

Delfont's deputy agreed to hear Frankie and gave him a one-night unpaid spot at the Kingston Empire in 1951. To prepare for it, he hired a cellar opposite to the Windmill Theatre where he practised the two songs he had chosen – 'Powder Your Face With Sunshine' and

'Pennies From Heaven'. He was late for the rehearsal at the Empire because he had not realised how far he had to travel. The pianist he had hired persuaded the producer to wait for him. At the first house, Frankie was a great hit and was promoted to number two on the bill for the second house. Delfont immediately hired him to do a tour with a Hetty King show. A week at the Hulme Hippodrome in Manchester, for which he got a £100 advance, followed. This was big money for someone who had nothing. Then the BBC booked him for two appearances on 'Variety Fanfare'.

Frankie was on his way to the top – or was he? For the next 18 months, except for occasional spots around the London area, no work came his way. By now Stella was pregnant and the landlord wanted them out of their flat. Frankie's luck changed just in time. An audition with HMV records led to a recording contract, which produced enough money to buy a flat in Hamilton Terrace, St John's Wood. After the publication by HMV of the single 'My Sweetie Went Away', Frankie's career took off in a big way. Over the years, he had 29 chart entries, including 'Garden Of Eden' and 'Tower Of Strength' as number ones.

From now on Frankie was never short of work. For nine weeks he was top of the bill on the national circuit of Empire Theatres, including Liverpool in May 1957. In the same year he was the Variety Club's personality of the year, appeared on the Ed Sullivan show as the highlight of a tour of the USA and made his first film. This was 'These Dangerous Years', directed and produced by the husband-and-wife team, Herbert Wilcox and Anna Neagle. The story line was about a soldier who deserts from the army and comes back to his hometown of Liverpool. One of the locations was the same Cast Iron shore that Frankie played on as a child. This was the first of a series of films. Then came 'Wonderful Things', the story of a fisherman in Malta. Next he starred alongside Anna Neagle in 'The Lady Is A Square'. The following two films were made in Hollywood – 'Let's Make Love', co-starring Marilyn Monroe in 1961 and 'The Right Approach'. When advances were made to him by Monroe, Frankie is reported as saying, 'I'm a very happily married man. My wife is my lady.'

In between times Frankie was on stage across the world, including most European countries, and with resounding success in Las Vegas in 1959. If he had been prepared to live in the USA, he would have made a fortune. Although Stella and the children, Andrew, David and

Susan, moved out there for a while, they were soon back in Britain. Part of the reason was that Frankie found the American attitude to Jews, of whom he was one, difficult to stomach. He found that the British were much more tolerant in their outlook.

By the 1970s Frankie was taking life easier, concentrating on one-off concerts and cabarets. A rare return to the stage came in 1985 in the London production of '42nd Street'. Along with his profession and his family, Frankie's great love was boys' clubs. This stemmed from his days in Lancaster. In his busy career he always made sure that he put aside a week to tours clubs throughout the country. Because they did a lot for him, he wanted to repay them. For example in September 1962, he was in Liverpool to help both the Florence Institute and Norris Green clubs. On his American tour in 1958, he found time to speak at the American Boys' Clubs convention, as well as appearing at the Royal Festival Hall in the NABC review. He eventually became vice-president of the National Association of Clubs for Young People. His services to youth were recognised by the award of the OBE in 1965 and the award of an honorary fellowship at Liverpool Polytechnic in 1988. In 1997 he became a CBE for his Boys' Clubs work. The *Liverpool Echo* made him the recipient of its Arts and Entertainment Award in 1998.

His great love of football led to him leading the singing of 'Abide with Me' and 'You'll Never Walk Alone' at the 1973 Cup Final. His lifelong anchor was his religious faith, which helped him to recognise some of the falseness of the showbiz world and heed the call to look after the needs of others. In May 1999 he underwent emergency heart surgery at the John Radcliffe hospital in Oxford. After a number of operations, he died on 17 September 1999, soon after returning home to High Wycombe. According to Jewish custom, he was buried on the same day.

# Norman Vaughan (1928- ) *2003*

For years Norman trod the boards as an ordinary run-of-the-mill comedian. All this changed one night, when he was appearing down the bill on the Lonnie Donegan show at the Winter Gardens, Blackpool. Val Parnell, the theatrical impresario, had slipped in unnoticed. He was looking for someone to replace Bruce Forsyth as compere of 'Beat the Clock' in Sunday Night at the Palladium. He decided that some-one was Norman. So Norman began a series of over 100 perfor-mances, which ended on 7 January 1962.

Norman's father Ben was a tailor by trade. When Norman was born, Ben and Nina were living with an auntie at 32 Barry Street, Walton. He had two sisters and one brother. Soon they moved to what was then 4 Lewlithia Park Road. It is now 36 Beach Road, Litherland. His father became a bookmaker. Norman went to the local school further down the road. His favourite moments, though, were spent in the Col-iseum Theatre in Stanley Road, where he first got a taste for the glam-our of the stage. Norman inherited his talent from his father, who was something of an amateur comedian. In his teenage years Norman ap-peared with Tom Moss's 20 Eton Boys touring group, a trio going un-der the name of Winn, Taylor and Cary, The Dancing Aces and Dudley Dale's Gang.

More theatrical experience was gained during the war years. After serving with the King's Regiment in Europe, reaching the rank of ser-geant, he was moved into the sphere of entertaining the troops. He met his wife Bernice, a dancer, on a boat taking them to do a show in Egypt. After the war, they went on a long tour of Australia. Back home, life became something of a struggle, going from agent to agent to find work. His career was saved by the offer of a long contract with a Bernard Delfont review. Interspersed with summer shows at Great Yarmouth and other resorts, Norman was able to make a living.

After his Palladium success, Norman was in great demand on TV, following Bob Monkhouse in 'The Golden Shot', then moving into pantomimes and on the club circuit. In 1969 he had role in the musi-cal 'No, No, Nanette' in Eastbourne. By now the family were living in Carshalton. He even achieved his ambition of appearing in serious roles in 'Boeing-Boeing' at the Royal Court, Liverpool in 1967 and as the jester in *The Tempest* at the same venue two years later. In the for-mer role, he was so nervous that he insured himself against forgetting his lines. He is still remembered for his TV chocolate commercial 'Roses grow on you'.

# Robb Wilton (1881-1957)

'Keep it going till we get there' was the request of Fire Station Officer Wilton, as he answered a call to attend a fire. The author discovered an old gramophone record of the sketch in a holiday cottage a few years ago, fortunately along with a gramophone on which to play it. It was sufficient evidence that the reputation of comic genius was well deserved.

Although there was little trace of a Liverpool accent in his broad northern vowels, Robb was in fact born at 81 Warburton Street, Brownlow Hill on 28 August 1881. He was christened Robert Smith. His father, Joseph, was a compositor with the *Manchester Guardian* and the old *Liverpool Courier*. Robb's stage talent was probably inherited from his mother Elizabeth who had been an actress. As a lad, he was an altar boy at St Mary's RC Church in Woolton.

After leaving school, there followed a variety of jobs – at Victory Engineering works in Tunnel Road, with a furniture manufacturing firm in St Anne's Street and at Turner's Nurseries in Garston. It was in Garston that Robb had his first stage experience at the Theatre Royal. But it was at the Theatre Royal in Breck Road, Anfield that he discovered his talent for comedy. The theatre was nicknamed 'The Blood Tub', because of the fairly violent four or five different melodramas it produced every week. Since changing the scenery between acts took a little while, Robb had the job of keeping the audience entertained during such intervals. He eventually found that his jokes were going down better than his performance in the plays.

After over three years at the Theatre Royal, Robb took engagements at the Lyric Theatre in Everton and the Pavilion Theatre, New Brighton. It was at the latter that the impresario Sir Walter de Frece, a Liverpudlian educated at the Institute, spotted him. From here, Robb's professional career took off at a great pace. He had found by now that doing long stints at one theatre took up too much material, so he decided to do mainly one-night stands, in spite of the extra travelling this involved.

By now he was married to Florence Palmer. Robb had met her while they were both appearing in the same play at the Alexandra Theatre, Hull. They married on 21 January 1907 at Holy Trinity Church in Stalybridge, Florence's hometown. Their first home was 3

Redcar Street, Clubmoor. The pair were inseparable over the years of their married life, claiming to have never spent more than a fortnight apart. In the earlier years they appeared together as a duo.

Over the next few years, the Wiltons spent half of the year touring in the United States, Canada and Australia, with the rest devoted to the London and provincial theatres. During one visit to Australia in the 1920s, Robb was told at a Melbourne restaurant that the chef could cook any dish requested. He asked for spare ribs and cabbage, a Liverpool dish he knew well. Imagine his surprise when the chef turned out to be a Scouser, who informed Robb he could only cook the dish if he had access to the spare ribs sold in Liverpool.

Robb's first broadcast was from Savoy Hill in 1922. In the 1930s, he appeared in two films with Gracie Fields, who incidentally had also learned some of her stagecraft at The Theatre Royal in Garston. But, like Tommy Handley, Robb became a household name because of his broadcasts during the days of the Second World War. His monologues began with the words, 'The day war broke out, my missus said to me' or 'my pal, Charlie Evans, said to me'. Charlie Evans was not an imaginary character, but an actual friend of Robb's who lived in Liverpool. After Robb's death, it was Charlie who made the suggestion of a memorial plaque in his memory.

Post-war, Robb inevitably began by saying 'The day peace broke out', but after the death of his wife in February 1956, he never used the phrase 'my missus said to me' again. His sketches included Robb in the role of a fireman, air-raid warden, policeman, Home Guardsman and football manager. An example of his patter comes from the last mentioned. 'The crowd kept yelling at us to go out and buy Stanley Matthews, but when I asked Charlie Evans if we could afford Stanley, he said that on gate money of 2s 4d a week, we couldn't even afford studs in the players' boots.' Robb's best-loved sketch, however, was his role as Mr Muddlecombe JP. In one particular portrayal, Mr. Muddlecombe was somewhat inebriated and asked a lady defendant for a drink in a pub afterwards. This immediately brought a complaint from the Magistrates Association to the BBC. It received an answer from the redoubtable Director General Lord Reith. He explained that since the charge against the lady in the imaginary case was of holding tortoise races in a 30-mile limit, he thought that the association might be lacking in a sense of humour.

Tragedy struck the Wilton family in the last year of the war. Their

*Testing, testing . . . The combined weight of music hall veteran Wee Georgie Wood, Merseyside MP Bessie Braddock and comedian Ted Ray at the unveiling of a seat in St George's Gardens, in memory of Robb Wilton.*

only son Robert, an actor, was accidentally killed at the age of 35. He fell from a window in a house in Maida Vale during a London black-out.

Robb continued to be in great demand in the post-war years, still topping the bill at the London Palladium as late as 1951. In 1955 he took a cameo role in Arthur Askey's film 'The Love Match'. As his wife's health deteriorated, Robb and Florence came to live with Mr and Mrs Breach in 30 Mayville Road, Mossley Hill. By now Robb was working only during the summer months. This gave him more time to devote to Liverpool. He became President of the Liverpool Archery Club, Vice-President of the Liverpool FC Supporters' Club, President of the Wavertree Community OAPs branch and played snooker at the bowling club in Church Road, Wavertree. After he opened a church Christmas bazaar in Wavertree, a woman came up to him complaining that his impersonation of Robb Wilton was not a very good one!

One of Robb's last appearances was at a charity concert on behalf of the British Limbless Ex-Servicemen's Association at the Pigalle Theatre, Liverpool. He said, 'I think I will make it my last show.' It was. He died in Broadgreen Hospital, his funeral taking place at St Margaret's, Anfield on 6 May 1957. In June 1959 a memorial plaque was placed on the wall of the foyer of the Empire Theatre. The inscription stated, 'To the eternal memory of Robb Wilton, born 28 August 1881, died 1 May 1957. A pillar in the foundations of the British music hall. Laughter was his life and life was his laughter.'

One newspaper suggested Robb nationalised his humour and his debt to Liverpool remains 'unrevealed and problematical'. Others were more generous in their assessment. Arthur Askey, who as a boy saw Robb at the Hippodrome said, 'He could make anything sound funny – even a telephone directory.' The slow, hesitating, lugubrious speech, the comical face, the wipe of the hand across the cheek needed to be seen and heard to be appreciated. He originated the phrase, 'To live in Liverpool you have to be a comedian.'

# Anne Ziegler (1910-)

The names of Ann Ziegler and Webster Booth went together like chalk and cheese. Romantic musical stars of stage and screen, the duo were the pre-eminent British matinee idols of their time. Not many knew that Anne was a trained opera singer.

Born Irene Eastwood at 13 Marmion Road, Sefton Park, the daughter of Ernest, a cotton broker, Anne had a nursery governess at home during the First World War. Her maternal grandfather, James Doyle, was a well-known architect in the city, designing many pubs and churches. The family later lived on Queen's Drive in Mossley Hill. From the age of nine to sixteen, she went to Belvedere School on the fringes of Princes Park. So-

*Anne Ziegler, the young opera and musical star*

cially, she was escorted by various young men to the subscription dances held at the Adelphi Hotel. She had lessons on the piano, but when the organist at her church, St Agnes's, Ullet Road, heard her sing, he suggested that she ought to take singing lessons as well. These were with John Tobin, who ran the Liverpool Repertory Opera Company. Entering the Liverpool Music Festival at the old Philharmonic Hall, she won a gold medal for singing a piece from the 'Marriage of Figaro' and silver for piano playing.

Dr Wallace was a well-known conductor at the time in Liverpool. Anne sang under his baton both in a first performance of Gustav Holst's 'The Wandering Scholar' and also at a St George's Hall Concert. In 1933 she gave a recital of music by Mozart, Beethoven, Handel and Walton in the old Rushworth and Draper concert hall. Her talents were displayed in the capital when she gave the same programme at the Wigmore Hall in London in the following year. The change from classical singing to musicals came when she took a small part in 'By Appointment', staring Maggie Teyte.

Irene Eastwood did not sound glamorous enough for a budding

*Anne Ziegler with Webster Booth, her husband, world famous for their duets*

star, so John Tobin suggested that she ought to change it. So Irene Eastwood became Anne Ziegler, the surname coming from a German expert on precious stones, who at one time lived on the Wirral. In December 1934 she played the part of Marguerite in the first colour film based on the opera, 'Faust'. The title role was taken by her future husband, Webster Booth. A return to Liverpool the following year saw her playing principal boy, alongside George Formby, in 'Mother Goose' at the Empire Theatre.

Taking part in a TV concert from the Alexandra Palace in 1936, a month after the start of television, was a highlight of Anne's career. Broadway fame called when she made her first visit to the USA. She sailed from Liverpool on the Cunard White Star line in 1937 to star in the musical 'Virginia'. Here she called herself Anne Booth, because of the American prejudice at the time against foreign names. Anne and Webster Booth married in London on 5 November 1938. The husband-and-wife team did four productions in London for George Black, the impresario, and two at the Blackpool Winter Gardens.

During the war years Webster and Anne took part in many variety, concert and radio shows, including some for ENSA. Their signature tune was 'Only A Rose'. As the war ended, they appeared together in 'Sweet Yesterday' at the Adelphi Theatre, London. In the same year, 1945, they sang at the Royal Command Performance at the Coliseum Theatre, London. A high spot was when one of the first foreign football teams to play in England, Moscow Dynamo, came backstage to meet them. In the winter of 1947-8, they were invited to sing at the morning service for the King and Queen in their private chapel in the grounds of the Royal Lodge. All the corgis were present for the sherry and biscuits in the Lodge drawing room afterwards. Sailing from Liverpool on the Blue Star line new liner, 'Imperial Star', Webster and Anne embarked on a nine-month world concert tour in 1948, visiting South Africa, Australia, New Zealand and Tasmania.

All through the years 1939 to 1953, Webster and Anne made many records with EMI. After a short tour of Canada in 1953, they lived in South Africa from 1956 until 1978. Now a widow, Anne lives in Llandudno.

# Bibliography

Jefferson, Alan. *Sir Thomas Beecham*, 1979

Kennedy, Michael. *Adrian Boult*, 1987

Black, Cilla. *Step Inside*, 1985

Hunter, Rita. *Wait Till The Sun Shines, Nellie*, 1985

Chegwin, Keith. *Shaken but Not Stirred*, 1994

Lister, David. *The Crazy Life of Kenny Everett*, 1996

Wynn, Barry. *Music In The Wind – The Story of Leon Goosens*, 1967

Grundy, Bill. *That Man – A Memory of Tommy Handley*, 1976

Moseley, Roy. *Rex Harrison: The First Biography*, 1990

Woodward, Ian. *Glenda Jackson*, 1985

Johnson, Holly. *A Bone In My Flute*, 1994

Miles, Barry. *Paul McCartney – Many Years From Now*, 1997

Guiliano, Geoffrey. *George Harrison*, 1993

Marsden, Gerry, *I'll Never Walk Alone*, 1993

Melly, George. *Scouse Mouse*, 1984

Moore, Ray. *Tomorrow Is Too Late*, 1988

Moore, Ray and Alma. *Tomorrow – Who Knows?*, 1989

O'Connor, Tom. *Take A Funny Turn*, 1994

Kenyon, Nicholas. *The Making of A Conductor*, (Simon Rattle) 1987

Stuckey, David. *Fried Bread and Brandy-O*, (The Spinners) 1983

Clayson, Alan. *Ringo Starr – Straight Man or Joke?*, 1991

Ziegler, Anne and Booth, Webster. *Duet*, 1951

Robinson, Robert. *Memoirs: Skip All That*, 1996

Collins, Pauline. *Letter To Louise*, 1992

McCauley, Peter. *Music Hall in Merseyside*, 1982

Wilmut, Roger. *Kindly Leave The Stage*, 1985

Mellor, G.J. *The Northern Music Hall*, 1970

Hudd, Roy with Hindin, Philip. *Roy Hudd's Cavalcade of Variety Acts*, 1997

# Also of interest:

## LIVERPOOL & THE MERSEY: A Nostalgic Pictorial Journey
*Peter Woolley*

"a beautifully illustrated book... many of the postcards reproduced in this splendid large-format paperback are in private collections which makes this collection of greater importance" The CHESTER CHRONICLE. £7.95

## WEST LANCASHIRE WALKS
*Michael Smout*

No need to venture into touristy areas, it's all on the doorstep for Lancashire's walkers – "Knowledgeable guide to 25 rambles by the Ramblers' West Lancs Group Chairman" RAMBLING TODAY. £5.95

## EAST LANCASHIRE WALKS
*Michael Smout*

The rambling reverend continues his revelations! This companion volume to "West Lancashire Walks" leads you to an abundance of walking and places of interest which lie just beyond your urban doorstep to the East – a haunted house near Warrington, an American Wood at Aspull, and there's even a giant on the banks of the Mersey! £6.95

Our books are available through booksellers. In case of difficulty, or for a free catalogue, please contact:
**SIGMA LEISURE, 1 SOUTH OAK LANE, WILMSLOW, CHESHIRE SK9 6AR.**
Phone: 01625-531035  Fax: 01625-536800.
E-mail: info@sigmapress.co.uk
Web site: http//www.sigmapress.co.uk
MASTERCARD and VISA orders welcome.